PACK AN
EXTRA PAIR
of
UNDERPANTS

George

So glad we found
each other,

Lead ON!

Michelle

Michelle Pallas, Inc.
www.michellepallas.com

ISBN 978-0-9895255-8-9

1. The main category of the book — Business Leadership. 2. Another subject category — Self Help / Personal Growth / Success. 3. More categories — Careers, Entrepreneurialism, Management, Professionalism, Mentoring, Coaching

Cover Design and Illustrations: Bart and Jessica Rinke
www.RinkeWebandDesign.com
Author Photo: Jennifer Dery, JoNa Photography
Manuscript Consultant: Linda Angér
Copy Editor: Dave Mesrey

PACK AN
EXTRA PAIR
of
UNDERPANTS
Leadership Inside Out

MICHELLE PALLAS

DEDICATION

This book is dedicated to my husband and life partner, Rick Pallas. Rick helped me to realize my dreams and showed me the power of believing in people. He patiently stood by me over the years as I learned what it truly means to be a leader. Rick is my very special personal guide and courage coach. If not for him, this story would have turned out very different.

CONTENTS

ACKNOWLEDGMENTS

This project was not at all what I expected. I started with an outline and a timeline. Being an experienced project manager, I was confident in my ability to deliver on time and within budget. And then I started to understand the creative process from the inside out. I experienced the impact of my guides and the influence of the people around me. Tapping my network to capture diverse perspectives, I'll be forever grateful for the honesty of friends and family. Fara Warner was my first editor, the person who encouraged me to let my story breathe. She inspired me to find my voice regardless of how uncomfortable it made me feel. I'm so very grateful for her persistence. Without her, this would be a boring business book instead of a motivational memoir.

I'm eternally grateful to Rick for reading a million drafts and hearing me ask, "Do you want to talk about my book?" every day for over thousand days.

Thanks to the creative team for their illustrations and cover ideas. They stuck with me while I relentlessly pondered possible images that both supported my leadership story and reflected my casual nature and determination. My sister, nieces, husband, and friends were all part of the project, but it was the Rinke team that brought it home.

Jesse will always have a special place in my heart. Not just because she created the hiker theme, but because she led me through the creative process. We're no longer just aunt and niece. She has advised and amazed me. We've forged a new relationship as adults, and I could not be more proud of the person she's become. I'll always be grateful for the total Rinke team commitment. If not for Bart's guidance, intense listening, stealthy contributions, and encouragement, I'd still be moving words around on these pages.

Thank you to my dear niece Jenny, a skilled photographer and creative artist.

To my editing team who, over and over, took the time to read and reread. Your feedback helped me make this my best effort. I love you all!

And to Dave Mesrey, who became an integral part of the book. With his high editorial standards, Dave constantly advocated for you, the reader. Throughout this journey, he became my mentor and writing coach. I'm grateful for his sense of humor, his risk-taking, and his commitment to excellence. It's been a powerful partnership, and I hope our hard work inspires a new generation of leaders.

ABOUT THIS BOOK

Unlike most memoirs, this book — in combination with the *The 7 Acts of Leadership Workbook* — also serves as a self-help guide when you complete the workbook activities. Or you can simply enjoy this motivational story on its own.

Michelle Pallas's *7 Acts of Leadership* are tried-and-true behaviors that, when applied consistently, play a critical role in determining your success. They are presented here in summary format, as well as throughout the book.

Act 1: Know where you're going
   Visioning and goal-setting enables realization of dreams

Act 2: Broker Capability
   Designing a network of talent requires knowledge of people

Act 3: Connect
   Making connections depends on a clear vision and a believable story

Act 4: Role Model
   Deliberately selecting and being a role model defines character

Act 5: Care
   The key to leadership

Act 6: Have Courage
   Bravely taking action after thoughtful consideration

Act 7: Live Right
   Choices made when no one is looking

Throughout *Pack an Extra Pair of Underpants*, you'll encounter little nuggets of wisdom called "laser lectures." These powerful "Pallasisms" were inspired during coaching sessions with the author's family, friends, and associates. Each laser lecture — followed by thoughtful contemplation — can be more effective than any long-winded lecture. A partial list of laser lectures can be found at the back of this book and a complete list at *michellepallas.com*.

Some of the names of the people in this book have been changed to respect their privacy.

JOURNEY OF A SEEKER

CHAPTER 1
LEAVING HOME

I watched the riots unfold from my front porch. I saw the tanks rumble down Mack Avenue, the smoke pour from the burning buildings, and the unmistakable sound of gunfire in the air.

Somewhere in America, it was the Summer of Love. But not here. This was a city on fire. This was Detroit.

Martin Luther King Jr. was assassinated, then came Bobby Kennedy. Then the Chicago riots. It was a tumultuous time in history. A tumultuous time in America.

Our fragile wood-frame house survived the summer of '67, but because of where we lived, we could no longer get fire insurance. We could no longer rely on the status quo. Detroit and the nation were in search of new leadership. A new philosophy. A new beginning.

By the time my eighteenth birthday rolled around, I wasn't thinking about what it takes to become a leader. And I certainly wasn't thinking about what it means to be an entrepreneur. I was too busy thinking about how to change my life so that I wouldn't have to live under the reign of my father anymore.

As a girl growing up in the 1960s and '70s, I was often the victim of gender stereotyping. But instead of embracing traditional roles like homemaker, nurse, or "girl Friday," I set out to find my own path, regardless of the consequences. I didn't have that "fire in the belly" often associated with a leader. I had no desire to lead others; I was too busy focusing on myself. An internal force was driving my desire for freedom from a father who led his family with a traditional command-and-control style.

And who could blame him? He lived in a man's world where women were subservient and men dictated the way it was, both at work and at home.

His world and mine could not have been farther apart in the 1960s. I grew up in the Dery family, learning from my five older siblings as they navigated their lives through a revolutionary time in America. I held my mother's hand while she sat inches from the television sobbing over JFK's assassination. I had never seen her cry before, and I wondered if it meant we would go to war. At school during "civil defense drills," we were taught how to survive a nuclear attack. "Duck and cover" made the Cold War a reality for us. The death of the president was a tragic, almost personal loss to my mother and a complete mystery to me.

I was on the tail end of a generation of baby boomers who made protesting war their job, peace their motto, and disdain for the establishment their weapon for change. In 1970, at the height of the Vietnam War, a protest on the campus of Kent State University came to a violent end when the Ohio National Guard shot and killed four students. Crossing the border to Canada to dodge the draft was a real consideration for my brothers and a source of shame for my father.

Middle-class America's deep family secrets were featured nightly on the evening news: equal rights, racial segregation, drugs, politics, religion, and sex. What was the world coming to? Traditionalists responded by denying that change was coming and that things just needed to get back to the way they used to be.

Day of reckoning

In 1975, our Thanksgiving Day dinner conversation wasn't about the nightly news; it was about the smell of the turkey and fate of the Lions. Our holiday meal was always served at the conclusion of the annual football game. Dinnertime discussion was dominated by my three older brothers, my Pa, and my grandfather, who were all reliving the play-by-play.

My two older sisters and Ma prepared and served the meal. My grandmother, Nana, lived upstairs. She made us dessert on holidays, which was the only time she ever came downstairs when Pa was home. She hated Pa. On this particular day, Nana would sit on the far side of the dinner table to avoid him. She hated his drinking, his smoking, and the way he got my mother pregnant every few years. But I was oblivious to it all.

With my eighteenth birthday just days away, I was under some stress of my own. I couldn't help but wonder if the rest of the family knew of the contract I'd negotiated with Pa when I was sixteen. I never spoke of it with my siblings; no one was there when it happened, except my mother. She knew. But she acted completely normal. A sports fan who'd been stuck in the kitchen all day, Ma was eager to hear the details of the football game, even though the Lions had lost.

Maybe I had imagined the big fight that took place two years earlier. Had Ma smoothed things over with Pa? If so, why had Pa not spoken to me for nearly two years? We lived in the same house, shared the same bathroom, sat at the same dinner table, yet we never spoke to each other after our heated argument about college.

I learned at an early age not to go directly to Pa for anything. Always present ideas to Ma first. So when my government teacher encouraged me to pursue college, I did my homework. I knew money would be an issue, but my parents helped my brothers and sisters. My oldest brother, Fred, was a graduate of the University of Detroit. Dave was a graduate of Wayne State University, and John was pursuing his degree there, as well. At the time of the big fight, my sister was pursuing a nursing degree at Mercy College. According to Pa, this was an acceptable profession for a woman.

It only made sense to me that I should get the opportunity for a college education, too. I had high hopes; I wanted to be a lawyer. I met with a school counselor, who told me I needed my parents' income tax information and their signatures in order to submit my application for government student loans. It was my junior year of high school, and many of my friends were already making plans for college. I was excited about the possibilities.

Every night, Ma sat at the dining room table watching TV in the living room, swilling her Stroh's and smoking her Viceroys. Pa sat in the kitchen nook listening to Ernie Harwell on his transistor radio. He would often sit and study subdivision blueprints, drinking his beer and smoking his cigarettes.

Ma and Pa never sat together.

When I was younger, I would sit in the kitchen with Pa and help him create home subdivision themes. We brainstormed street names: Camel, Winston, Pall Mall, Marlboro, Salem, and Viceroy. The cigarette subdivision was just one of our creations.

But this was not one of those nights. Ma gave me the okay to talk to Pa, and I gingerly slipped into the kitchen, each step an eternity. I told him how badly I wanted to go to college, about my dream of becoming a lawyer. I handed him the loan application and pleaded for his help. In order to determine my eligibility for a student loan, Pa would have to sign and complete the forms.

Looking back now, I can see why a law degree might have seemed farfetched to Pa. I probably shouldn't have brought it up in our first discussion about how to pay for college. Maybe my expectations were unrealistic. I had no way of knowing that my siblings all worked their way through college without help from Pa. It didn't matter; what happened next changed both our lives forever.

His response reverberated in my head like a rock slide in a cave:

"You're too stupid to be a lawyer."

I was dumbfounded. In Pa's mind, I wasn't worthy of an education or a career. Even if I *were* stupid, what kind of father says that to his daughter? Parents are supposed to nurture their children, not shatter their dreams. I felt betrayed. Who was this man? I hated my father at that moment. My head quickly filled with rage, but I simply stood in silence, wondering if he was right.

My grades were great. My teachers loved me. I represented the student body on the curriculum board, providing feedback to the faculty council on course improvements. I represented my class on the joint faculty-student judicial board. I was no dummy.

I pondered Pa's response. So what if I was stupid? I thought. Didn't I deserve the same chance to get an education that my siblings had? I asked Pa if he would at least fill out the forms so I could just see if I qualified for financial aid.

"Don't I deserve a chance?" I asked.

"You're a girl," he said. "You don't need college."

This didn't make sense to me. Pa's traditionalist mindset was colliding with my new-age views, where women had careers and went to college for an education — not to bag a man. I grew up watching *Mary Tyler Moore* on TV, and my teachers were liberal antiwar activists.

"So you're saying you're not willing to help me get a degree?"

Even if Pa couldn't — or wouldn't — help me financially, I needed his moral support. I wouldn't give up, and my persistence angered him. Pa remained motionless in his chair as if to restrain himself. Suddenly, the blood rushed to his face and he raised his fist. "You will do what I tell you, or you will leave this house now!"

Bam! His fist hit the table.

For the first time in my life, I was afraid of Pa. I slunk backward out of the kitchen, eyeing him as I growled, "You're legally responsible for me until I'm eighteen."

Those were the last words we exchanged for nearly a decade.

I learned something about the traditional role of women that night. Returning to the dining room where my mother sat listening, I begged her to talk to Pa. But my plea fell on deaf ears.

"What Pa says is the final word."

And so it was. That Thanksgiving Day, just three days before my eighteenth birthday, would be the last time I celebrated a holiday with my family in that house. There was no indication that anyone besides me knew this was a possibility. I cleared the table just as I did every night after dinner. My sister Pat washed while my sister Mary dried, and I carefully returned the dishes to the china cabinet where they would sit until Christmas. I wondered who would put them away after I was gone.

My eighteenth birthday was a cold and sunny Sunday. Detroit's first black mayor, Coleman Young, was still in his first term, planning the construction of a riverfront Renaissance Center. Down along the Potomac, Michigan native Gerald Ford occupied the Oval Office, picking up the pieces of Watergate.

6

As usual, Ma went to early mass so she could get home in time to make Pa his bacon and eggs before noon services. By the time she got home, I was in the driveway packing up the Pinto.

I'd bought the old blue hatchback from my brother John, who sold it to me for all the money I'd saved working part-time for an ad agency downtown. Twice a week, after my morning bookkeeping class, I caught the Cadillac-Harper bus down to Simons Michelson in the Lafayette Building. Riding the city bus in those days was an education in self-defense. I quickly learned that when you stand on the bus, it's best to position yourself where the perverts can't reach up your miniskirt.

Whenever I had to maneuver my way to an empty seat on a crowded bus, I always had to do so strategically to avoid getting groped. I eventually learned to appreciate these lessons, but at the time it was terrifying.

I usually arrived at work just in time for the switchboard operator to take lunch, leaving me a tangled mess of cords, which ultimately resulted in a lot of disconnected calls. It didn't take long for me to be relegated to the typing pool.

I was glad to give John my life savings in exchange for some freedom. He taught me to drive a stick shift on the only street in Detroit with a hill: Ashland. John coached me while the old Pinto rolled backward down the hill until I got the feel of engaging the clutch while simultaneously accelerating. It was a decent car, but it didn't have much room. Still, space didn't really matter at the time. I didn't have much to take with me.

I wished things could've been different. I was disappointed, especially in Ma. I wondered why she didn't seem to care about me. I wondered if she thought the whole thing had blown over and that everything was normal again. Maybe my parents just didn't understand that I was really leaving. But I was of legal age, and I was finally responsible for myself. I was scared.

Before I just drove away, I needed to know if my parents knew I was really leaving. I'd give them one last chance to say, "I'm sorry, Michelle. Will you stay and see if we can work this out?" I asked Ma if I could take my bed. She said she'd ask Pa.

Inside my head, I was screaming at them. "So if I leave, is that a relief to you? Why did I ever want to reconcile with you?!...*I hate you!*"

I stood silently in the dining room awaiting Ma's inevitable answer. I was on the verge of tears, but tears were a sign of weakness in my household, and I fought them back. Finally she returned.

"No," she said.
Simple as that.
I should've known.

Without so much as a goodbye, I walked out the door. I wanted to hide in the basement, but I accepted the consequences of questioning Pa's authority. I was bound and determined to show them I was far from stupid, even if it killed me.

I had no plan. For months, my friend Maureen and I had talked about getting a place together so we could share expenses. We even had an apartment picked out. But when push came to shove, Maureen backed out. The last thing I wanted was to move into my boyfriend's parents' house. But that's what I did.

Tony's parents welcomed me with open arms. When I arrived, Tony proudly showed me the upstairs dormer, which would serve as my bedroom. His dad insisted that I have my privacy and threatened to shoot Tony if he even thought about sneaking upstairs after dark. The space had been used as a storage attic, and plenty of work went into cleaning it up. Tony and his brother even put on a fresh coat of paint. I never had my own room before. I truly felt special.

I was ashamed of where life had taken me and embraced this new beginning. It was the complete opposite of what I'd left behind. Was it possible that these people who barely knew me actually cared about me? I questioned the possibility, but accepted their kindness.

All work and no play

I found a job as a typist downtown for the accounting firm Peat Marwick. I quickly poured myself into it and worked overtime every chance I got, taking every opportunity to learn from the professionals at the firm. I was especially intrigued by the business consultants, who seemed to have much more fun on the job than the auditors and tax accountants. I was already daydreaming of becoming a consultant someday.

My job was going pretty well, but without a college degree, I couldn't make a career of it. Starting at the firm as a statistical typist, I gradually earned more responsibility and eventually came to supervise a small team of typists. In the 1970s, the world of professional services was still very much a man's world, and female role models were hard to find. Still reeling from my mother's response to my plea for help, I was determined to find a confident woman who could successfully handle the politics of the workplace. I would watch and learn, just like I'd done all my life as the youngest of six.

I soon developed an interest in technology when Marge asked me to help evaluate the newly invented word-processing machine as a possible replacement for our IBM Selectric typewriters. The investment was a big decision for the firm's partners, and she was creating a business case.

Marge was my supervisor's manager. She was a middle-aged woman with a real presence about her. When Marge entered a room, you knew she was there. No one was invisible to her. She managed by walking around, and everyone in the typing pool feared and respected her. The professionals did, as well. They looked up to her as a shrewd businesswoman capable of managing the Detroit branch of a national accounting firm. Marge was in charge.

Her story was believable. The state-of-the-art new word-processing products were necessary to keep up with technology and for us to remain competitive as a firm. She also knew that experience with new technology would be impressive on a résumé. As it turned out, this was the first of many adventures I would have with software package selection projects. This smart, sophisticated lady showed me how to make decisions, propose a solution, and secure funding amid a sea of politics. Marge had a vision, and I was her lieutenant. I was learning, and my loyalty made me privy to her change strategy.

Once we finished our product evaluations, Marge knew that getting funding for the solution we wanted would be a challenge. The partners were real tightwads — a characteristic I later came to appreciate as an entrepreneur. Marge prepped me like a lawyer preps a witness. We ran through the benefits of the new system and found real-life examples to use on upcoming jobs. While we waited for approval of the purchase of our new machines, typists were trained to communicate the benefits of new technology to consultants, principals, and partners whenever the opportunity presented itself: "If we had a word processer instead of electric typewriters, the changes you need could be ready in an hour instead of a day." Our typing pool was the "social media" engine of its day.

When the partner-in-charge of the firm showed up asking about the new word processors, Marge was ready with the approval for him to sign. This was my first lesson in the power of informal communications and navigating change in organizations. I imagined getting that signature must have been what it feels like to win a case as a trial lawyer.

While I was actually having fun at work, my personal life was in shambles.

After living under my boyfriend's parents' roof for a year, I felt pressure from Tony's family to get married. Living together as a couple was still frowned upon in 1976, and it was time for us to get our own place. Tony's sister made all the wedding plans and, before I knew it, my wedding day had arrived. Against my father's wishes, all my siblings and their spouses came to the wedding. My brother John gave me away.

The invitation was addressed to my parents, and my sister Mary assured me they got it. They did not respond. I stood with John at the back of the church. Everyone was seated, and it was time for me to walk down the aisle. I wondered if my parents were sitting out there in a pew. I made John go into the church to look. He shook his head.

"They're not here," he said. "You're disowned, just like I'm gonna be for walking you down the aisle."

He joked, trying to make me smile. But again I felt betrayed. I gave Ma and Pa a chance to be parents, to join me in a life celebration. They refused.

I was determined to make it a joyous day, so I put them out of my mind and walked the walk.

We moved into an apartment across the hall from my brother John and his wife, Cathy, an old multifamily structure on the east side near Alter and Mack. Tony and I had one of two apartments on the second floor. John and Cathy had the other. That year went by fast, and I enjoyed having the company of family just steps away.

I continued to be banished from Dery family gatherings, which only brought me closer to Tony's family. John and Cathy would report on Dery family matters after their holiday gatherings, and we would all laugh about how everyone secretly talked about me behind Pa's back.

At work, thanks to my efforts on the word-processing project, I was promoted to supervisor and Marge became my boss. Tony was working as a butcher at a meat-packing company. We both worked plenty of overtime and soon we had a down payment for a two-family brick home, affording us a source of rental income. At least that was the plan. Still hopeful for a higher education, I enrolled in a business-law course at the community college but found myself missing classes when Tony kept disappearing with the car.

It wasn't long before Tony lost his job — on account of an alleged work "accident." We began to grow further and further apart while I worked six days a week trying to keep up with the bills. I avoided going home. While on disability and painkillers from his accident, Tony decided to join an outlaw motorcycle club and started taking part in underworld activities — behaviors I found unacceptable, but easy to deny while I was consumed with work.

I had become a victim, trapped in a world I'd created for myself. Maybe my father was right, I thought. I was twenty years old and in a state of ignorance, naiveté, and depression when the phone rang. It was my sister Mary. Mary was ready to go on vacation and willing to pay my way. I was wallowing in my misery, too ashamed to accept her offer and afraid she'd see right through me. I was harboring a secret: My marriage was a huge mistake, but I was too proud to admit my parents were right.

Mary insisted that she'd be the one to benefit from a vacation. She sold the idea as if I was doing her a favor. But the truth was she was already on to me. She knew I was trapped, and she wanted to help me out. I reluctantly accepted her offer.

Our trip out west brought us together as adults. Our family policy growing up had been to hide our feelings, to ignore conflict, and to sweep things under the rug. But we were on an adventure now, just the two of us, headed west to bask in the beauty of America's national parks. It was liberating. For the first time, we openly talked about our childhoods, sharing stories both happy and sad. Together we were questioning why and why not. We talked about religion, politics, and family secrets.

By the end of our vacation, I was no longer the little sister and Mary the big sister. We were women doing the best we could with the cards we'd been dealt. We returned home not just sisters, but friends.

Mary didn't change me. She didn't pull me from my state of hopelessness. I did that. But what she did was monumental. Mary created a setting where it was safe for me to think about living my life differently and to put my thoughts into perspective. She gave me a backdrop for dreaming about life's possibilities and considering my potential. I was finally ready to shed my victim mentality and take ownership of my actions. As a result of our time together, I opened my own door to change.

Through the majesty of the Grand Canyon and the spirit of Yosemite National Park, my passion for life was reignited. Mary showed me that she'd be there for me, without judgment. I could trust her. She cared about me, even when I did stupid things. It would be years before I really understood the power of the gift of caring. But at that time in my life, when I trusted no one, I accepted her hand with a promise to be there for her, as well.

Lessons in trust, accountability, and change were yet to come for me in the context of leadership. But the foundation for my character development was now in place.

I arrived home to a mess. A garbage can filled with empty pizza boxes blocked the front door; beer cans were scattered across the living room floor. As I waved goodbye to my sister, our Doberman Pinscher, Magnum, greeted me at the door. A bag of pot sat next to a roach clip in an ashtray on the table. An empty bag of chips lie on the floor, obviously finished off by the dog. A small mirror and razor blade were the only things on the dining room table, which was pushed to one side of the room. We often moved the table like that when we had parties so our guests could easily move from the kitchen to the living room.

It was three o'clock in the afternoon, and Tony stumbled out of the bedroom yelling that I wasn't supposed to be back until later in the day. He was right; Mary and I had caught an early flight home. In all of my naiveté, I'd hoped for a joyful reunion. I was hopeful that Tony would be surprised and glad to see me after a week away. He was surprised, all right, but he was *not* glad to see me.

It was a raw and emotional homecoming. I didn't want to let go of the euphoria of my vacation. I refused to acknowledge his yelling, and I ignored the messy house. My focus turned to unpacking, laundry, and getting ready for Monday morning at work. I could no longer deny my circumstances, and I made my decision. This chapter was about to come to an end. All I needed was an exit strategy. A vision for my future — and the steps to get there.

I returned from my trip with clarity and focus. I was no longer in a state of depression and hopelessness. Not getting a divorce because I thought my parents would "win" was crazy. The divorce was a foregone conclusion. But this life change was far different from when I left my childhood home. How I handled the divorce was a matter of my very survival.

Learn to say 'That's unacceptable'

Prior to my vacation, Tony and I argued often about his drug use and his shady friends, and while he threatened to, he never physically abused me. We distanced ourselves from each other. I stayed at work late and, before long, he stopped coming home at night. For this I was thankful.

But I was constantly on edge because Tony sometimes showed up without warning to pick up his tools in the basement or to use the garage. Taking refuge in the library down the street, I felt safe. There I wrote out my goals, just like the self-help books suggested:

1. Get a divorce by the end of the year
2. Start night school at the community college

Writing down my goals made them seem possible. I researched how to get a divorce. I read that before seeing a lawyer, it's best for both spouses to talk through their issues in an open manner. But by that point, an open dialogue with Tony was impossible. I immediately rejected the advice.

Child custody and visitations were a large part of every book I opened, but that wasn't a concern for me. I knew from the beginning that my marriage was a means to an end, and having children with Tony would ruin my chances of living my life my way. I was well aware of the impact a child would have on my life because of a babysitting experience I had when I was barely thirteen.

I was twelve when my nephew Dennis was born in August of 1970, and three months later I found myself responsible for him while my sister Pat was vacationing on a catamaran in the Caribbean with her husband, Jim. They couldn't get any farther away. There were no cell phones, emails, or instant messages in 1970. If there was an emergency, it would require a ship-to-shore radio transmission — an expense I'm sure wasn't in their travel budget.

It was a perfect plan in Patty's mind: Get little sister to babysit. Ma was only a phone call and three miles away. Everything I needed was right there in the house, and Ma could check in once a day. What could go wrong?

Well, for one, I couldn't get Dennis to stop crying. Exhausted at the end of each day, I set him on the floor between the television and me and let him cry until one of us fell asleep. He cried for six straight days. We both cried. I could see why my sister wanted to get as far away as possible.

During that week, I had time to reflect on her situation. My sister was forever tied to the responsibility of raising Dennis. Her husband had a good job and would most certainly be a good provider. She'd quit her secretarial job downtown and was now a full-time stay-at-home mom. It was the dream of every little princess, a script that had been written for her and women before her since the dawn of time.

Looking back, I find it odd that my mother never expressed any concern about Dennis's crying. She'd raised six children, and this seemed a normal occurrence to her. Was she trying to teach me something? Was this a cruel lesson about birth control? Or did she want me to experience what she already knew to be my fate? I didn't know if she was preparing me or just trying to warn me. All I knew was this was *not* for me, and I vowed to find another path. I didn't want to be dependent on a man, and I sure didn't want to be responsible for a child.

If it's important, leave nothing to chance

Every night after work, I went to the library to read. There was an entire shelf of books dedicated to the topic of divorce. Now, as I learned how to get a divorce, I was thankful for my mother's lesson and found humor in the gift that Dennis gave me. Not having children simplified the process for me. A significant portion of every book was dedicated to child concerns. Topics ranged from how to tell the kids to negotiating for child support. I was glad I didn't have to worry about any of that.

The steps seemed simple: Get a lawyer, file the papers, show up in court, and get on with your life. I was confident I could manage that. But I needed more answers.

How was I going to escape my marriage without getting hurt? I left the divorce books on the table and wandered over to the psychology section. I pulled a heavy textbook from the shelf. Introduction to Psychology. I stopped at the section about coping with stress and returned to my table.

I devoured every word about behavioral theory, intelligence, perspective, aggression, drug dependency, patterns of abuse, depression, personality disorders, coping with threats, and what it means to be "normal." Time stood still as I immersed myself ever more in the book. Next thing I knew, there was tap on my shoulder; it was the librarian, and she startled me. The library was closed. She glanced at my stack of divorce books and gave me ten minutes to collect my things.

I was energized by my newfound knowledge. I was starting to understand my situation and myself, but I needed more time to research before I could hatch an escape plan. I was learning a new vocabulary that explained my life experiences, and I was starting to realize I was not alone.

The library became my haven. It was the place where I figured out that my childhood is what happened to me, but it was not who I am. Amid the whispered voices and smell of books, I felt safe. As I learned about personalities in books like *I'm OK, You're OK* and *Games People Play*, I discovered similarities between Tony and Pa. Making sense of my world was empowering. It was liberating. At the same time, it was also shameful. I was embarrassed by the thought that I might have been a victim of emotional abuse.

This new awareness was the catalyst I needed to challenge myself to change. To *really* change. Not just to get divorced but to re-create a healthy life for myself, one void of threats and filled with possibility. Breaking the cycle would require a complete reinvention. I had to find a way to use my past as a strength and to generate a positive force to carry me forward.

I didn't have a natural network to nurture me, so I had to create one. Suddenly filled with hope for the future, I wondered how I could use my existing relationships to help me safely escape from my marriage. The only person who could manipulate Tony was his dad.

Salvatore was a traditionalist, just like my dad. A man's house is his kingdom. The man is the provider and disciplinarian. But Sal was different than Pa in his attitude toward guns. Sal always kept a pistol nearby. Sometimes, when arguing with his kids, he'd threaten to pull it out from under his La-Z-Boy.

Tony was living with his girlfriend, and Sal was concerned about him. He was also ashamed of him. Tony was a drug addict and far from being a provider. Months earlier, I met up with Tony's brother, who told me to stop Tony from taking drugs and straighten him out. I was both amused and amazed that he thought I had such power.

I was studying the psychology of guilt. I was starting to understand its powerful grip and the impact it had on me as a child growing up in a Catholic household. I decided to use it to appeal to Sal's provider instincts.

Our conversation was short and without contest.

I knew he'd be home alone, and when I arrived it seemed like he'd been waiting for me. I was surprisingly unemotional and confident. "I need your help, Sal. I'm going to file for divorce, but I'm afraid Tony will get violent when I serve him papers."

Sal didn't even look at me. He just stared at the TV and took a slow drag on his Camel. "Are you sure of your decision?

"Yes" I said confidently.

Sal remained focused on the TV, never once turning toward me.

"Has he ever hit you?" he asked.

I hesitated to answer. I didn't want Sal to think there was no real threat and that I was overreacting.

"No." I said. "He's hit the wall, thrown things, but he's never actually hit me. But his drug use has changed him, Sal. He always carries his gun. I don't trust him or the people he's hanging around with. He's not the same person you raised."

Sal was visibly upset. He took another drag on his Camel. "If anything happens to you," he said, "I'll kill him myself." I turned to go, and he faced me for the first time. Tears welled up in his eyes. "Be sure to tell him that."

I left wondering if he would keep his promise, and knowing that it wouldn't do me any good if I was dead. I did take comfort in knowing that I had Sal's blessing. That was big. But now the word was out, and I had to be ready for anything.

Later that night, I was in the kitchen making myself dinner when Tony showed up to pick up some things. Immediately I felt the tension in my shoulders, and my heart began to race. Adrenaline rushed through my veins. "I met with a lawyer this week," I said. "I need an address where he can serve you your papers."

I saw his face harden and his right hand land on his hip. "You did what?" he said. "Are you crazy?" He tossed the kitchen chair across the floor. "I'll never give you a divorce!"

I needed to keep the conversation from escalating. "Settle down," I said. "You know this only makes sense." I should've stopped there, but I made the mistake of saying, "Besides, now you and your girlfriend can get on with your lives."

We had never openly talked about his girlfriend. He paraded her around in front of friends and family like a trophy. He had no shame about their relationship. But today, he was angry I brought it up. I needed to say something fast.

"Your dad told me to tell you he supports my decision."

Tony's voice cracked. "You told my dad we're getting a divorce?" His expression changed as he considered what would happen now that his father knew. He started looking around the room as if he was searching for something.

"Dad wanted me to let you know," I said, "that if you hurt me, he'll kill you."

I didn't know if Sal would really back that up, but I needed to buy myself some time.

Tony reacted with silence — a really long silence. I watched for a spark of understanding to blanket his expression, but I only saw bewilderment. Again, he looked around the kitchen like he didn't know where he was. I spotted a knife on the counter next to an onion I'd been cutting. I quickly looked away.

My heart was racing. I'm not sure if I waited a second, a minute, or an hour. Tony stormed out of the house without a word, slamming the front door so hard the wood cracked. I was afraid he'd come back. I quickly packed my work clothes and fled.

Because Tony and I didn't have children, the process of divorce was primarily administrative. At that point, I wasn't sure if my success or my survival would be my revenge. Survival was my priority. I left nearly everything in exchange for my life.

Over the next ten months, while I waited for our divorce to be final, I moved twice and changed jobs in order to dodge Tony's threats. When he called me at work, I hung up. When he showed up at my office, I called security. When he left me voice messages telling me I'd never be safe, I erased them. One terrifying night, I cowered in the corner of my apartment while Tony tried in vain to break down the door.

ACT 1: KNOW WHERE YOU'RE GOING

Look into your soul to find your vision.
State your goals with eloquent precision.

Refer to *The 7 Acts of Leadership Workbook* to complete your own vision statement and set your goals. The worksheets are modeled after the self-reflection exercises I used at this stage of my life to redesign my future. The guidelines enabled my very reinvention. I continue to use them today to help me refine my road map. The examples offer guidance as you map your future, writing down your career, life, and community goals. Keep your goals fresh by reflecting, refining, and rewriting them throughout your life. Act 1 activities include goal-setting and writing a vision statement.

CHAPTER 2
STARTING OVER

The time had come for me to start anew. I'd finally begun to understand myself and why I'd made some of the decisions I made. I had to tell myself it wasn't all my fault. That I wasn't stupid. That just because my marriage had failed didn't mean *I* was a failure.

I came to realize that the past was something I couldn't do a thing about. That looking back was valuable, but only if I learned from my mistakes. I had to stop living in the past and start living for the future. To be honest with myself about where I was in my life. To craft a new reality. Otherwise I couldn't truly start over.

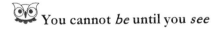 You cannot *be* until you *see*

I had a sketchy vision for my new life, but who did I want to be? Getting a divorce and enrolling in college were huge victories in themselves. But now I wanted to put the past behind me and reconstruct my DNA. That meant creating a new reality for me. I had to find the tools to lead myself. I began setting goals and painting a new canvas. I was both excited and terrified. But I was finally ready for personal change.

I committed to two goals: behave consistent with my desired character and deliberately surround myself with people I admire. But first I had to figure out what I wanted my character to be.

My reinvention continued at the library, reading every self-help book I could find. Books on destructive patterns, depression, codependence, self-esteem, personal worth, and forgiveness helped me to understand my choices. I learned that I was a product of my environment and how my victim mentality was holding me hostage. I promised to practice a positive attitude. I decided to take a cold, hard look in the mirror and start practicing some new behaviors.

Later, the book *Your Erroneous Zones* would guide me in shedding my victim mentality.

Understanding the power of affirmation, I began jotting down notes in a small calendar I kept in my purse: "I am not a victim," I wrote. "I am a survivor." I retraced the statement every day. I didn't think of myself as a leader, but as someone who would have a greater positive impact on others than any negative influence people could have on me. "I am worthy of happiness," I added.

These were just baby steps, but they put me on my path to personal worth.

I began to study successful women at work. "What makes her an educated, successful, and independent woman?" I'd ask myself. "How can I be like her, surrounded by a rich network of talented people?"

I understood that in order for me to successfully reinvent myself, I would not only have to change who I was, but I would have to teach people about the new me. First, I needed to reflect on my character. The journey couldn't truly begin until I envisioned who I wanted to be.

I wrote down a whole page of adjectives describing this imaginary person: dependable, trustworthy, responsible, smart, fair, confident. I wanted to be surrounded by a rich network of talent; people with capabilities beyond mine. Just like a runner who trains with athletes who challenge her, I was seeking people with the right behaviors so I could be challenged while absorbing their positive energy.

In my research, I learned that we start to model our behaviors after our parents and family at an early age. When we start school, our friends and classmates then begin to influence our thoughts and actions. The behaviors of these role models feed our character.

Knowing my family history was an important step in letting go of my past and moving into my new world. It would be years before I realized the true impact of being the child of alcoholics. But I was becoming aware of the impact of my childhood experiences. Guilt, anxiety, embarrassment, confusion, anger, and depression fueled my struggle with trust. I was starting to accept that my five brothers and sisters might have had more to do with raising me than my parents. I was okay with it, and I set out to redefine my course. It wasn't until much later I would find strength from the healing words of John Bradshaw in his book *Family Secrets*.

Surround yourself with people you admire

To make sense of my reinvented network, I defined four groups of people: aliens, natives, guides, and villagers. Then I used my network to change myself in ways both subtle and significant. I was beginning to understand the impact of role models. First, I ditched everyone who was toxic to my new thinking. That meant alienating friends I had made jointly with my ex-husband. That was easy. I severed all contact with them when I fled for my life. No one could be trusted.

Next, I wrote a list of people I admired. At the top of the list were my siblings. Family members are natural residents of your network; they're natives. You can move them into alien status when their behaviors are toxic to your goals, but you can't really get rid of them. My brothers had been raised with gender stereotyping, and I needed to manage that perception by re-engaging them in my life, not as a little sister, but as a confident woman.

My parents belonged to this elite group of natives, as well. I had alienated them, and they had alienated me. I knew I had to find the courage to repair the relationship. But I wasn't ready.

Marge was my first work mentor. When there was conflict over priorities, staff schedules, or client requests, she masterfully facilitated a resolution. She deliberately took the time to build relationships across the firm. She had the respect of everyone, even if they disagreed with her.

Never take your network for granted

I lost touch with Marge, but her actions were imprinted on my mind. I wanted to be like her — a skillful, courageous communicator. I vowed to keep people like Marge in my network from then on.

My list was short. I had basically alienated all my friends, and outside of family, my village consisted only of coworkers. I felt very much alone, unsure that my natives would buy into the "new me." I needed courage coaches and guides, smart people who believed in me and who would provide sound advice.

Depending on others for my mental well-being was a terrifying thought. I was on the threshold of a new way of life, but I was intimidated by the thought of developing relationships. I didn't know what a healthy relationship even looked like.

My coworkers were definitely smart and confident, and appeared to be fair and dependable. I had been keeping them at a distance, too ashamed to tell them my life story. But now it was time to consider these residents of my network as possible mentors. I was looking for people who could help me make good decisions. I needed advice about college, what classes to take, what programs to pursue. I wanted people in my network who would encourage me to succeed, who would challenge me to be the best I could be. But I didn't know who I could trust.

How do you know if you can trust someone? Can you tell when you first meet them? Does it take days, months, or years to know for sure? What exactly does it mean to be trustworthy? How would I develop this characteristic in myself? I only had questions. No answers. In the short term, I decided I'd be very cautious while I figured it out. After what I had been through, I doubted I would ever trust again. But I had to try.

With my desired character in mind, I began to strategically draw people into my network as guides to help me reach my goals. I hoped to be able to do the same for them someday. To do this, I had to understand what they were capable of, not just where they worked or where they went to school. I scheduled time every month to sustain or grow these relationships, and I continued to read my books. One of the best was Dale Carnegie's *How to Win Friends and Influence People.*

🦉 We teach people how to treat us

My first order of business was to devise a plan to reengage with my natives. Introducing the "new me" to my siblings was a personal marketing campaign. I was the black sheep of the family, so I set out to rebrand myself. I packaged up a nice little message and individually visited each of my five siblings. "The divorce is final. I have a new job. I'm attending night school. I'm growing up. I want you in my life, but you need to respect me for who I am, not what I was."

Admitting that I needed other people to achieve my goals was humbling. Fred, my oldest brother, loaned me money to pay for night school. Each week, part of my paycheck went to pay him back. I was building character, being responsible, being dependable. But no sooner was my debt paid then it was time to borrow again for the next semester.

John and Cathy, my brother and sister-in-law, offered me a safe place to live. Mary, my sister, helped me repair my relationship with my parents. For the first time in a long time, I wasn't alone in this temporary experience called life.

My siblings were glad to have me back. At that point, I had seven nieces and nephews. I knew I could get a free meal by watching kids, and they could get a break from parenting. Sometimes I even got some homework done, too. My brothers and sisters became my courage coaches.

In the meantime, my father's health was failing, and my mother had become his full-time caregiver. Pa and I politely greeted each other and exchanged meaningless conversation about the Tigers and the nightly news. But the hard conversation about what went wrong still lingered. I wanted to talk, to clear the air, but the words just wouldn't come.

My presence at family gatherings brought a sense of relief to Ma. The whole family was together again, and I was especially grateful for my time with the kids. I was becoming aware of my influence on my nieces and nephews as a mentor. I was free of the rigors of parenting, but I still had a direct effect as a role model. I wondered if they were aware of the tension between my parents and me. I wanted something better for the kids. I wanted them to know that being dependable and trustworthy was an expectation for both a child and a parent, and that ignoring something doesn't make it go away.

But how could I teach it if I wasn't living it? I knew the best way to teach right from wrong was to lead by example. I had to show my parents that they could trust me, that they could depend on me. I had to let go of the past once and for all. And even though I still felt they'd let me down, being there for my parents was the right thing to do.

I was changing my DNA. I was reinventing myself. I felt compelled to break the cycle of generations, to be a person my nieces and nephews could rely on. I would inspire them to be the best they could be. I would show them they could trust me. History is an important element of change, and I had to be honest about the current state of affairs in order to move forward. I had to forgive my parents. I knew this in my head, but I still wasn't ready in my heart.

Passing the torch

As my vision for a new life came into focus, I started to wonder about my grandparents. Why was Pa so angry about life? What made Ma so complacent when her mother was so independent? My sister Mary could remember my parents having card parties with relatives and friends when she was young. I had no memory of it. Having people over to the house had suddenly stopped, and we couldn't help but wonder why. Growing up, my friends were never allowed in the house when Pa was home. I just accepted it.

Mary and I decided to make a project of documenting the family tree, seeking to uncover some hidden truths. We started by interviewing Ma. She freely gave us information about her late sister Betty and what she knew about my grandmother's family. We delighted in stories about her childhood and learned more about what happened when her father died during the Great Depression, leaving my grandmother to manage his rental properties and raise two girls on her own. Her dad's brothers were inventors and entrepreneurs who came from Boston, previous generations having left Ireland during the potato famine. Her mom's ancestors came from Germany in the 1800s and settled in Michigan as landscapers and florists. She claimed her great-grandfather even invented the long-stemmed rose. Her great uncle, Philip Breitmeyer, was a florist and one of the founders of the Florists' Telegraph Delivery (FTD). And from 1909-10, he was mayor of Detroit.

We then asked Pa about his family history.

"It's none of your business," he answered.

This perplexed us. What made Pa so secretive? Was there something in his past he was ashamed of? I knew his mother was a victim of the 1918 flu pandemic, which rendered her physically weak and mentally compromised, dependent on her siblings for care. When my dad wasn't away at boarding school, his aunts raised him in a big house across the street from my grandfather's hardware store. But that didn't seem like reason enough to shut us out.

His response, of course, piqued our curiosity. My sister Mary and I both wanted to know how we "fit" into the world. It wasn't until years later that we discovered my father's rich ancestry. We slowly peeled back the onion of time that eventually led us to Montreal and Quebec City. We discovered that our ancestors were among the early settlers of Quebec, arriving from France in 1658. As the generations migrated westward, they eventually settled in Detroit, where they bought narrow divisions of land called strip farms. Each property offered narrow access to the Detroit River, about 250 feet, and these strips of land were up to three miles long.
We never uncovered any embarrassing secrets to account for my dad's reticence. Perhaps they're yet to be discovered.

Eventually, a sense of pride would come from learning about these great pioneers and community leaders. Out of their legacy would come inspiration for my community giveback activities but not until much later in my journey. I learned that acknowledging the past is an important element of change as an individual, as well as an organization. My personal search enabled me to appreciate the importance of this step when I began leading change for others later in life.

Discovering my heritage was an exercise in understanding myself. I chose nuggets from my ancestors' lives to incorporate into my vision of myself. I was no longer starting from zero. I would now build upon the dreams and accomplishments of my forefathers.

 If it's important, leave nothing to chance

We buried Pa on November 8, 1985. I was 27. The wind whipped cold against my face and my legs as we followed his casket down the steps of Saint Clare.

During the service, I sat next to Mary and quietly sobbed while my mother kept stoic. She seemed completely accepting and comfortable in the moment. I had regrets. My opportunity for reconciliation was gone forever. My emotional detachment had slammed into the wall of reality. In the bitter cold at the foot of the church steps stood my brother's wife, Sandie, who held me while I sobbed.

"I'm not crying because he's gone," I said.

"I know," said Sandie. "You'll never reconcile now."

She held me tight, and I began to shiver.

Pa had taught me lessons about society's traditional expectations of men and women. From him I'd learned much about myself and my inner drive for change. But perhaps most of all, Pa had allowed me to understand the power of trust and the fragility of words. And because of this, I vowed never again to wait for the other person to start a critical dialogue.

In search of answers, I read books about forgiveness and healing relationships. One day I sat down and wrote a letter to my deceased father, explaining why I felt betrayed and how I wished things would've been different. I forgave Pa. I forgave myself, as well. I put that letter in my desk drawer, where it sits to this very day. Occasionally, when I'm melancholy, I still read it.

I understood that holding a grudge against my father would only hold me back. So I refused to succumb to negativity. There were many things Pa provided for which I was grateful:

- A private Catholic education
- My brothers and sisters
- The roof over my head
- Trips up north in the station wagon
- Fun times at the kitchen table after dinner making up street names
- Spontaneous stories about a puppy dog and a pussy cat
- Poetry readings

Through this simple exercise, I was able to put aside my anger and bring voice to my conversation with my mother. Just a few weeks after Pa died, Ma and I sat together at her kitchen table in the small apartment where she lived alone. Just like old times.

She was smoking a Viceroy but now she was drinking a Busch. I was nervous. Starting the conversation was hard, but I'd made a promise to myself.

"Why do you think things happened the way they did between Pa and me?"

Ma hesitated before answering. She adjusted her seat but refused to look at me.

"We made mistakes when it came to you," she said, finally. "Your Pa didn't understand how determined you were. We both agreed that we made mistakes."

It was too painful to dig any further than that. I'd hoped for an expression of sorrow, an explanation for not coming to my high school graduation or my wedding. But the questions would only be torture for us both, so I accepted her words.

"You know, Ma, I'm going to be here for you from now on," I said. "You can count on me."

I didn't want her to feel the pain of loneliness that I had felt.

"One thing is true," she said. "We never stopped loving you."

We both cried that night. That was all we ever said about it, but the conversation gave me license to put the regret and the anger behind me. For that I was thankful.

Ma and I never became good friends, but we accepted each other for the life choices we'd made. I respected her choice to accept her role as a traditional housewife, and she respected my never-ending search for a better way.

ACT 2: BROKER CAPABILITY

Surround yourself with people you admire.
Your network will grow as you desire.

The 7 Acts of Leadership Workbook section on Act 2 provides a character plan, a network plan, and a network assessment. These activities helped me weed out the people with whom I no longer wanted to associate. I also uncovered courage coach candidates who helped me recover from some bad habits. Surrounding myself with the right people gave me the energy I needed to achieve my goals.

CHAPTER 3
DEVELOPING YOUR CHARACTER

My life was finally turning around. In just a few short years, I had accomplished plenty. I was happy with who I'd become and dreaming about my first real job when I found myself distracted by one of the accounting professionals at work. Next thing I knew, he asked me out on a date.

Memories of my past failures consumed me. I was focused on achieving my career goals; there was no room for a man in my life. Like many wounded women, I was "done with men" anyway. I dated a few times after my divorce, but the relationships were short-lived, as I learned my brother was right: Men have an obsession with sex-thinking. I was certain I would never have an intelligent conversation with anyone of the opposite sex when a coworker said to me one day, "Why don't you just let Rick be nice to you?"

Her words spoke volumes. I realized that my opinions toward men were showing through. Just because I'd been a victim of gender stereotyping didn't make it okay for me to do it back to men.

My goal was to be confident, but I was afraid that I would re-create the trap I'd made for myself when I was eighteen. I was still harboring some serious trust issues. I didn't want to live in fear of relationships. I strived to be the best I could be at managing myself and my relationships with others, and I wanted to be a positive role model for my nieces and nephews.

I couldn't grow or be that confident person without taking some risks. Rick was educated, clever, polite, handsome, and fun to be around. He was also a certified public accountant. Maybe he could help me with my tax return! Besides, it was just a date. It wasn't like I was going to marry him.

Finding my courage coach

I soon found myself enjoying Rick's company and taking his advice about school. He was practical about his goal-setting and smart about his finances. He coached me by asking questions about my dreams and helped me formulate ways to reach my goals. Believing in me even when I doubted myself, he encouraged me to apply for scholarships. This guy was a breed I had never encountered. His belief in me gave me the inspiration to keep chasing my dreams.

Rick quickly became both a guide and courage coach. I was beginning to trust again, and I cautiously fell in love.

My attitude about men was changing, and my stereotypical views were being challenged by this new relationship. According to Merriam-Webster, a stereotype is "something conforming to a fixed or general pattern; especially: a standardized mental picture that is held in common by members of a group and that represents an oversimplified opinion, prejudiced attitude, or uncritical judgment."

The reason we categorize people into groups is to make sense of a complex world. My world had changed — and it was *because* of Rick, not in spite of him. With him at my side as my partner and friend, I was becoming the best I could be.

This was a revelation for me. I reflected on how my experiences had shaped my assumptions about men. My childhood filters no longer applied. My reality had changed, and how I interacted with my world needed to change. I started to wonder if there were other areas of my life where I jumped to conclusions about people just because of their gender, the way they looked, or how they talked. Understanding my natural preferences became critical to my reinvention.

 Stereotyping is never the right thing to do

I'd been a victim of gender stereotyping many times, but that didn't give me license to do the same. I was wrong to lump all men into the category of useless and controlling non-contributors. The time had come for me to have an open mind about the people around me. My attitude would be my weapon for change. Again, I contemplated my character plan.

I wanted to be known as someone who's dependable, trustworthy, responsible, smart, fair, and confident. But was I really being fair? I added *nonjudgmental* to my list, hoping it would get me closer to my goal. In order to be fair and nonjudgmental, I had to be the best I could be at listening.

As my nieces and nephews grew up and new ones arrived, I wanted even more to be the best role model I could be. I focused my attention again on my own character-building. I knew it was important to spend time with the kids, so I set a goal to see them at least once a month and to be the best I could be at listening.

I knew that tracking my goals and celebrating my accomplishments was key to becoming a successful businesswoman. It was the secret to my uniqueness. I started keeping track of my wins in a "victory log." Sometimes it was a simple task: "submitted application for scholarship." Sometimes it was a milestone: "graduated from college with honors." Each victory was the result of knowing where I was going and deliberately engaging my network to get there.

At the end of each year, I compared my victory log against my goals. I also considered my character plan. I was looking for needed development when I remembered that I wanted to spend more time with the kids. There were no entries in this section of the log. I'd failed to meet my goal. This is why goals should be written down. Like sand filling the space between rocks in a jar, my available time was filled with random tasks blown in by the wind. After a year of only wishing I was spending more time with the kids, I gave myself a lecture that I'd given them so often: You'll never have time unless you make time — and if you really want to change, you have to share your plan with someone.

You'll never have time unless you make time

The most important people in Rick's life were his parents; they were his guides. What I found most interesting was that Rick was also a guide to his parents. It was a two-way coaching and mentoring relationship that crossed generations. It was a form of reverse mentoring. This fascinated me. Later, I would apply the concept to my relationships, but at the time I was merely a student. I observed the relationship with a bit of envy. I was learning how healthy families interacted, and that included weekly visits to Gus and Virginia's home. In the beginning, I was just a witness to their meaningful dialogues over dinner. But before long, I became a part of the exchange. They asked my opinion and showed interest in my dreams. We connected.

Two other important guides in my network were my brother John and his wife, Cathy. They were the ones who took me in when I had no place to go and helped me get back on my feet.

Cathy didn't judge; instead, she listened. When life came crashing down around me and I was paralyzed by fear, Cathy was my anchor. She didn't hesitate to welcome me into her home and into her heart, even though she worked midnights as a nurse while raising two boys. My brother John and I solved lots of problems together as we separately searched for our places in the world.

John and Cathy accepted me into their family unconditionally. I found myself helping raise their boys, Johnny and Mike, doing laundry, making dinner, even installing insulation in the attic. One weekend, I watched the boys so John and Cathy could get away. Nine months later, Bethie was born at home. I stood beside the boys, my brother, and the midwife while Cathy gave birth. She invited me to attend this very special event, a gift for which I'll be forever grateful. It was as close as I'll ever get to experiencing childbirth, and I was okay with that.

Cathy was studying to be a nurse midwife. She wanted to give mothers the option to have their babies at home. So here she was eating her own dog food, as they say. After a successful delivery, Cathy went on to deliver hundreds of healthy babies at home. A leader in alternative medicine, Cathy blazed a trail for modern-day midwifery.

Later, both Rick and I would attend the home births of Jesse and Danny. Sharing in these miracles brought us closer together, a memory that has bonded us for life. Rick helped me to realize the need to make these important people a priority. I got serious about spending time with John, Cathy, and their kids. It became more than just a mental note. It was time to make good decisions about how I spent my time — and committing to spending my time on the things that mattered.

Around this time, I also started to fulfill my obligation to check in on my mother once a week. My actions were finally syncing up with my goals. My confidence as a role model was really starting to grow when things suddenly went haywire.

Good advice gone wrong

One of my character goals was to always remain open-minded and nonjudgmental. But one of my nephews routinely challenged me. Dennis was a senior in high school when my sister Patty grounded him for coming home drunk. I listened. I was certain that telling him not to drink would be a waste of oxygen. So I focused on clarifying questions to help him think instead of telling him what to do. At the time, I was reading about coaching skills and the power of Socratic questioning and decided to use my new learning.

"Are you aware of the consequences of underage drinking?" I asked.

He was, but only to an extent. We talked about the possibility of getting pulled over, getting into an accident, or going to jail. We discussed the possibility of him killing himself, or, worse, killing somebody else. I advised him not to get in a car with someone who's been drinking and, above all, to never drink and drive.

"So if I have to make a decision," he said, "should I drive home drunk to meet my curfew or stay the night at a friend's house?"

"Stay with your friends," I said.

Dennis's mother, Patty, is fifteen years my elder. She basically raised me. So when she called, it was like a parent scolding a child. She was very upset with me. "Dennis said you told him to get a hotel room so he could party all night long with his friends after prom," she said. "He said he didn't need to come home until he sobered up."

Clearly, I needed to work on my communication skills.

I was becoming more and more aware of the need to understand how my words would be interpreted. Intellectually, I understood the process of communication: The sender packages up a message wrapped in her own personal filters and transmits it to the recipient, who unwraps the package using his own filters. Chances of getting it right are higher when people's backgrounds are similar. Age, education, and perspectives influence the wrapping and unwrapping of the message. That's why really important messages should be delivered face-to-face.

It didn't seem like it should be that hard to get it right. But it was. I let Patty yell at me without defending myself. At the end of our short conversation, I got my two cents in and asked, "Are you glad he wasn't killed in a car accident?" She said nothing, and we hung up without another word.

I took full responsibility for the miscommunication and set out to learn from my mistakes.

Something I was doing wasn't working. Even though I might say something with good intentions, Dennis nevertheless interpreted it to fit his needs. And in this case, Dennis's "needs" were something I failed to take into consideration.

My success at work and home depended on my figuring this out. And so began my quest to better understand the communication process. It started, of course, at the library. There I read books on personality profiles and communication styles. And because practice is the only way to develop a new skill, I began by experimenting on my family. I made my family complete personality assessments and adjusted my communication style to meet their preferences. I immediately began to see positive results.

My research was fruitful, and my ability to communicate was improving. But I had yet to learn how to truly *connect* with people. I needed to step into their shoes to anticipate what they'd do with the information.

I learned that strictly following results from personality profiles and communication-style assessment tools cannot take the place of using your brain. Sometimes, following all the right steps should be overridden by common sense, your gut, your instincts.

Verifying that a communication is received as intended takes work. But when the message really matters, it's well worth the time. If I had asked Dennis what he was going to do with the information I'd given him, I might have been able to uncover his plans. My gut told me Dennis was up to something when he asked about driving home drunk, but I didn't act on my instincts. Even perfect communication can fall short in the absence of trust. Dennis didn't trust me with the knowledge of a prom after-party. I couldn't blame him.

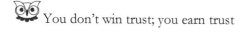 You don't win trust; you earn trust

Maybe it was too late or maybe the timing just wasn't right to establish a connection with Dennis. But John's kids were still young, and I wanted them to know they would always have a place to go when life got hard. I knew they'd turn to us only if there was trust. I understood the importance of it, but I still didn't know how to manufacture it. I suspected that consistent behavior and investing time were the keys.

First, we made a point of just being with them. When we scheduled a visit, we arrived on time, sending the message that if you want to be known as dependable, you do what you say you'll do. We set boundaries and held ourselves accountable. We called out unacceptable behaviors and spoke in terms of consequences instead of threats. We rewarded the kids with special trips that they helped plan. We did things that made memories and developed their self-esteem.

Sometimes Rick came, and other times it was just the kids and me. We spent the weekend backpacking with the boys on mosquito-infested Manitou Island. Nearly the whole family hiked the Ammonoosuc Ravine Trail to the top of Mount Washington in New Hampshire. When Jesse graduated from high school interested in the arts, just the two of us went shopping, visited art museums, and saw a play in New York City.

Together we went on road trips to Kentucky Horse Park, Ohio's Cedar Point amusement park, and other destinations. We stayed up all night watching movies on sleepovers. We went to concerts, afternoon teas, breakfast, lunch, dinner, and coffee. On a girls backpacking adventure, I took Jesse and Bethie to the national parks where I found my inspiration as a young woman. We backpacked to the bottom of the Grand Canyon and forty miles in the High Sierra Mountains, where we became more than family; we became each other's guides.

Over the years, we've worked out together on the stairs at Bloomer Park, walked the trails at Stony Creek Metropark, and rode our bikes all over town. We took part in many Multiple Sclerosis Society fundraising bike tours in the fight against a disease that personally affects our family.

We were building a bond of trust.

Trust came from sharing dreams, listening to one another, showing vulnerability, having an opinion without judging, and by caring enough to say "no." It was through our laughter and tears and unspoken words that our bond developed.

Trust doesn't come just from the passage of time. Trust develops as we observe one another and learn how we react to one another. It's a series of tests. We challenge our ability to hold a confidence and we wait, and watch, to see what happens.

Because we were dealing with the lives of children, we established confidence guidelines. The kids knew that all things shared with us would be held in confidence unless we felt they were putting themselves at risk. Our promise was to tell the kids about our concerns first before going to their parents. That promise was a communication protocol and part of our rules of engagement.

Developing trust is just one of the many lessons I learned from my nieces and nephews, and I would soon learn it to be true at work, as well as at home.

My communication style was evolving. I practiced being agile, adapting my style to meet the needs of others. I discovered that my preference for direct communications and my expectation of immediate results was offensive to some people. My drive to solve problems quickly led me to develop the bad habit of interrupting others. I needed to assess other people's communication preferences before speaking so that I could adapt my style as necessary.

Of course, I needed practice, and there was no better laboratory for experimentation than with my eleven nieces and nephews. I set my goals:

- Stop interrupting others
- Listen intently so that I can summarize the conversation

Committing to a new behavior, I shared my goals and gave my guides license to call me out when I interrupted them.

To help me stay focused while I was on the phone, I'd start doodling on note paper, journal pages, or sticky notes. Starting in the center of the page with a smiley face, I'd capture key points around the face. I ended with a pictogram of our conversation, a mind map. This enabled me to quickly summarize the conversation before hanging up.

Laser lectures

When the kids called me, I listened. In some cases, that was all they needed. Other times, I offered a bit of advice, something without judgment. Later, I would learn to ask permission to share advice from one of David Rock's coaching books. But my advice had to be easy to remember and immediately actionable. After all, they were just kids, and kids have short attention spans.

Every once in a while, I would actually say something profound. Amazed by my own brilliance, I would jot it on my doodle page and toss it in a hanging folder inside an antique metal cabinet I got from Rick's aunt and uncle when they retired.

When Rick and I got married, Aunt Marge and Uncle Harry became members of my native community. They served as entrepreneurial role models. An independent trailblazer, Aunt Marge continues to inspire and amaze me to this day. I was thrilled to have a piece of their history in my home office to remind me of their fifty years of successful business ownership. I still take comfort in how that old cabinet sounds like a cog railway when you open or close it. *Kla-kunk. Hmmm. Kla-kunk. Hmmm.*

As the years passed, I began to recognize recurring themes. The folder expanded. Each time a call came in, I listened while I searched through sticky notes, envelopes, and journal pages seeking an opportunity for reuse. The natives were on to me before I realized it. I know this because Bethie called one day because her brother Johnny told her to call me and ask for the lecture on surrounding yourself with people you admire. *Kla-kunk. Hmmm. Kla-kunk. Hmmm.*

Through all the mentoring and coaching experimentation came a growing list of reusable lectures, targeted reminders on how to live life. I was building a unique connection with each of my nieces and nephews, and I shared my insights because I cared about them.

But at the end of the day, I knew that all the coaching in the world couldn't take the place of an individual's drive and passion — a lesson I would soon take into the workplace.

JOURNEY OF A PATHFINDER

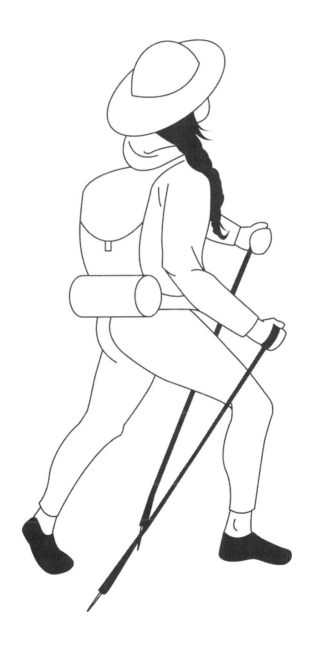

CHAPTER 4
MANAGING TO LEAD

Immediately after earning a degree in computer information systems, I landed a job as a mainframe programmer in the computer systems department at Kmart. It was an incredible opportunity and what I considered my first "real" job. The company was staffing up for a redesign of their item master database and merchandise systems. The programming language was COBOL, and the mainframe computer was king.

I was one of twelve college graduates to start our new jobs on the same day. Together, we attended a three-month training program to learn how to do our jobs using company processes and software tools. Working through team projects, we became friends. I welcomed them into my network, surrounding myself with smart people. In the years to come, we would all support and challenge each other in different ways.

My career as a programmer was short-lived. I was competent at writing computer code, but I was better at team-building. Maybe my manager saw my potential as a leader, but I doubt it. Being a supervisor had little to do with leadership. Leadership is about having a vision and taking followers to a future state. My promotion to supervisor was about getting the work done, period. However, it was definitely an entry in my victory log.

The job called for management skills. I was responsible for prioritizing work requests into a list and matching the assignment with the best available worker. Then I simply rode herd over everyone.

My new supervisory job proved easier than getting my COBOL programs to run properly when I was a software developer. Organization was a skill I learned early in life. Growing up in a house with one bathroom and eight people, every day needed to be well-planned and even better executed. We all knew that it was nine steps between my parents' bedroom and the bathroom door. It was just enough time to wipe your butt and get out of there when you heard them coming. Process efficiency and creative scheduling were second nature to me.

Management is the ability to get work done. It requires organization of work and team development. At the time, I had a task-focused management style. I was short on compassion and long on results. My coworkers openly called me "Callous Pallas." I admittedly needed work in the area of people management; regardless, my annual performance reviews were impressive.

Building a winning team

Every team has a life of its own, its own personality and way of getting things done. In order to breathe life into our group, I needed insight into the capabilities of each team member. I was searching for talent gaps. When I'd find a person skilled in an area that another person was lacking in, I'd simply match them up.

Designing a team competency map, I wrote down a few strengths and weaknesses for each team member. I used the information to establish knowledge-transfer opportunities by pairing one person's strengths with a person needing development in that area. In order to ensure a good match, I needed to validate my assumptions and inquire about team members' desires. Once the matching was complete and the coaches understood their roles as mentors, we addressed the gaps in talent through training or staff augmentation.

What I learned from the supervisory job was that matching the right work to the right person generates positive energy, and when learning becomes a part of each day, amazing things begin to happen. Creating opportunities for pairs of people to solve problems together builds team cohesiveness and individual self-esteem. What's not to like about that?

Accidental leadership

After climbing a few rungs on the corporate ladder, I found myself responsible for supporting hundreds of mainframe programs, a laundry list of new projects, tons of change requests, and nineteen programmers. As I took on more team members, I found success with my team mentor matchup. But soon I began to encounter problems assigning the work.

I inherited a team policy for on-call support that just didn't make sense. A small group of somewhat disgruntled employees supported our systems at night and on weekends. I suspected this was a case of more work being the reward for good work.

That's when I stopped being a manager and started becoming a leader. I envisioned the whole team working together to teach each other new things so that everyone could share the responsibility of on-call support. Work could be assigned to the next available person instead of the only knowledgeable one. Pairing people for coaching and knowledge transfer was working pretty well during work hours, but it didn't address our on-call inequity issue. I decided we had to change our way of assigning on-call responsibilities.

But when that decision was met with resistance, it posed my first real challenge as a supervisor. When I was just managing the work, things were okay; I was simply assigning tasks. But as soon as I proposed a new way of doing things, some team members became nervous.

"It'll never work," they said. "Sarah will never be able to handle a support call at 3 a.m." This was coming from the same person who was complaining about being the only one on call for that system. It defied logic. I was baffled.

Constantly trying to fix things by improving communications, I set out to clarify my message. My idea just needed further explanation, I thought. I wrote a detailed email explaining the new schedule and encouraged everyone to respond with their concerns. But no comments were forthcoming.

Analyzing the silence, I researched each team member's communication style preferences. It was pretty easy, since most team members were analytical programmers with a preference for detail. My idea was to document an on-call procedures manual. I even posted process flowcharts outside my cubicle. I scheduled time on everyone's calendar to conduct cross-training, and I asked everyone to update their performance objectives to include a knowledge transfer goal.

Yet after all that, nothing happened. The chosen few remained on-call using the old schedule, and cross-training fell victim to higher priorities. I'd told my team what to do, so why weren't they doing it? It was obvious my command-and-control leadership technique wasn't working. Demanding change simply led to resistance.

What I'd failed to take into consideration was the *process* of change, the human element that I knew so well from my own reinvention. My team members were in denial; they were avoiding me. Maybe some people were experiencing frustration, but they hid their emotions from me. If I could steer the conversation to the bargaining stage, at least there'd be some hope of finding a new way forward. I was on the brink of learning that people follow the vision, not the leader.

I found that managing work was easy compared to managing change. I reluctantly accepted that maybe I couldn't change my team, but that I could change me.

The only thing you can change is *you*

I decided I needed one of our team members to serve as guinea pig, so I called on Jason. I asked him pointed questions about his experience with off-hour production support. I collected data on how many calls he took and how long he was on the phone. He told me how often he had to drive in to work to fix the problem and how it was affecting his home life. Keep in mind, this was before the Digital Age. The only people with cell phones back then were doctors and drug dealers, and the only ones with remote access to computer systems were the government.

Jason explained what he did to solve the problem the last time he was called, and I put myself in his shoes. I connected with his reality. Laying out my vision for the team, I described a future in which everyone shared on-call responsibility. I took notes while Jason explained the forces that worked against my vision. I listened without contest.

I thanked him for his candor and asked if we could pick up the conversation again in a week. I wanted to hear more about his ideas and explore ways to address our challenges. During that week, Jason managed himself through every stage of the change process: denial, anger, bargaining, and depression — and, finally, acceptance. When we met again, Jason had begun to devise some new ways of working. He'd begun training Sarah as his backup. Together, they'd been reviewing issue logs each morning and walking through problem resolution. Jason challenged Sarah's decision-making, preparing her to support the production environment.

The following week, they were scheduled to share on-call responsibilities. Jason, together with Sarah, figured out how to make the vision a reality. He didn't need me telling him how; he just needed the ability to envision how he fit into the new state. Jason latched on to the vision, and I learned a lesson in change management.

Through a simple but meaningful dialogue, I was able to connect with the person who was critical to making the change a reality. This time I got lucky. I didn't know it at the time, but Jason was my change agent. He was the person who others watched; he was their role model. Once Jason was on board, the rest of the team seamlessly bought in to the new ways.

I was finding ways to turn my vision into a believable story.

"I'm not just managing people," I wrote in my victory log. "I'm leading change."

ACT 3: CONNECT

Words make a difference when changing thoughts.
Connecting with your audience is a gift to be sought.

Being the best communicator is important, but it's not enough when it comes to leading change. So often a lack of communication is blamed for the failure of projects. Organizations invest significant energy in evaluating the "who, what, and why" of communication breakdowns. But when it works, nobody notices. When it's working, there's a mysterious force that hovers over the team, department, or enterprise. Information is fluid. Teams self-monitor to keep everyone on the same page. Many team members communicate without even talking. They have a connection. Refer to *The 7 Acts of Leadership Workbook* to complete your own communication assessment.

CHAPTER 5
THE KEY TO LEADERSHIP

I was succeeding with team building, managing change, and coaching, but I was still searching for the secret to leadership. By now, starting my own business was in the ten-year plan. But I knew there was something missing from my management and leadership style that was keeping me from truly connecting with people.

Virginia's secret

Rick's Mom, Virginia, was retired from Michigan National Bank, where she spent thirty-seven years serving their customers as a teller, a supervisor, and eventually an assistant vice president. I wondered if she had any pearls of wisdom to share.

"What was the key to your career success?" I asked.

Her response: "I cared about people."

I quietly waited for her to say more. Was that it? I expected her to say it was her knowledge of banking, financial management, or her supervisory skills. To her, the answer was simple, but it hit me like a ton of bricks. I interviewed Virginia for hours about this topic until I thought I really understood what she was talking about.

She explained that caring about people isn't about giving presents or doing things for them. It's about listening with your heart, not just your ears. It's about empathy. It's giving hugs and letting tears flow, even if you're at work. It's about sharing your thoughts and feelings as a remedy, not as a burden. It's about being authentic and trustworthy.

I reflected on her words. Secretly, I questioned myself. Maybe I didn't really care about people because I was so absorbed in proving that I was smart enough to go to college. I was ashamed to admit that I really didn't care about the people at work. I really only cared about producing results. This new behavior would be hard for me because I was still living my life behind a protective emotional shield, and I feared that caring would be seen as a weakness.

I wondered why the people around Virginia didn't see caring as a character fault. Was there something special about her that made this behavior a strength rather than a weakness?

Virginia was born in 1915, the oldest of five children. Her father died when she was just fourteen, and she never finished high school. She divorced her first husband at a time when women simply didn't get divorced, especially not Catholics. She never used her two children as an excuse, but instead used them as her inspiration. Her second husband became her courage coach, just like her third son became mine.

But here was this woman who knew very well that if she had been a man, her career would've been different. She wasn't resentful; she was proud. She commanded respect, yet knew to pick her battles. She was a defender of what is right, yet tolerant of different views. She didn't find a path to follow; she blazed a trail for generations after her to find their way.

🦉 Care enough to take the time to know people

Virginia's ability to care was her strength because she balanced it with accountability. Caring doesn't mean you let people get away with things. It means you care enough about them to take the time to know them, to really understand their dreams and abilities. Sometimes it means helping them understand the consequences of their actions. It always means speaking with them on their terms, not yours. Meeting them where they stand. It means taking the time to help them think things through. Listening and providing guidance.

There's no greater gift to give than to care.

Virginia described all the things I was to my nieces and nephews, none of which I lived at work. She knew the secret to leadership. Leadership isn't about having all the answers; it's about helping others find the answers. She didn't think she was better than her workers, her boss, or her customers. She didn't have an exaggerated sense of her importance. She just saw a better way to do things at work that included careers for women, and she was willing to risk being herself at work, at home, and in the community. There will always be people who see caring in the business world as a weakness, and that was okay with Virginia. She simply chose not to cultivate relationships with those people.

Virginia became my role model in forgiveness, my mentor in caring, and my coach in leadership. I decided to start caring about people at work. This would prove to be my first real step toward a leadership lifestyle. The lines between work and home were becoming blurred. Maybe — just maybe — caring was the secret ingredient for connecting with people.

CHAPTER 6
LIFE AS A ROLE MODEL

In the beginning, there was no master plan to leverage diversity for the sake of innovation and team development. I simply had a curiosity about the way people live, their cultures, and the way they think. I was raised in a segregated neighborhood surrounded by people who looked like me and attended the same church.

In the workplace, I encouraged team members to share their backgrounds. We had potluck lunches where everyone brought traditional ethnic dishes to share. Together we enjoyed Indian samosas, Indonesian sweet ginger tea, Italian lasagna, African-American soul food, Polish kielbasa, and Jewish poppy-seed pastries. We celebrated everyone's holidays; showing respect was a norm in our team's work culture.

As it turned out, the sharing fostered team cohesiveness, and I was thrilled to have positively influenced the team dynamics. This was worthy of a victory log entry.

Breeding a leader

Even with the team camaraderie, there was still occasional conflict. This was especially true during program code testing, when everyone depended on each other to produce a quality system test. The test results provided assurance that our group of applications worked across multiple computer platforms.

Program developers are very proud of the code they create, and everyone had a sense of ownership about their works of art. At least that's what it was like back when mainframe computers were king and COBOL programming language was mainstream. So when Connie finished her unit testing, she passed her files on to Meeta. Both of them expected the software program to run flawlessly. But that was not the case.

Over the cubicle farm walls, I overheard mild-mannered Meeta's conversation with quick-tempered Connie. Meeta was trying to explain the problems she had testing Connie's data files. Connie's voice, at first just loud, quickly became shrill.

Meeta had a reputation for paying close attention to detail, and I could not recall her work ever being called into question. I also knew that standing her ground against Connie took courage. I would not have blamed Meeta for being afraid. Connie was on the defensive and refused to let Meeta finish explaining why her test wouldn't work. I quickly intervened. I simply insisted that Connie show some respect and let Meeta explain herself.

Connie and I were good friends. We started our jobs on the same day and attended the three-month corporate training program together. We played softball on the company team in the summer and volleyball in the winter. We rode together in bike tours, and our families vacationed together every summer. We weren't just colleagues, and Meeta knew this.

As a leader, it's sometimes necessary to manage conflict even if it means pushing back against your friends. So I politely did just that. Connie retested her program, fixed the bug, and that was the end of it.

One Saturday morning during a software upgrade, Meeta appeared at my office door. It was her day off so I was surprised to see her.

"I came in to work because I want to thank you," she said.

I was puzzled. It had been months since the incident, and I had completely forgotten it.

"You said that I knew what I was doing," Meeta explained. "You told Connie to re-examine her software program test results, even though you two are good friends."

Then she said my response had inspired her to enroll in a leadership program.

Right before my eyes, Meeta was developing confidence. That was the moment I realized the importance of inclusion and the necessity to manage conflict even if it means pushing back against your friends.

For a moment, I wallowed in my pride. I was not only proud of Meeta; I was proud of myself. I thought it was really cool that my actions inspired her to be the best she could be. In turn, her words fueled my desire to be the best leader I could be.

People are listening

After Meeta left, my sense of pride quickly turned to concern as I began to wonder what else I had said that others might have overheard. Had I said things I shouldn't have said? I wondered if I had a positive or a negative influence on others. This scared me. Who else was listening to me? Who else had I influenced?

This was a defining moment for me. It must be what it's like for a mother when her child repeats something she'd said. Sometimes it's good and sometimes it's bad. Being a role model comes with responsibility. I considered my impact, both good and bad. The importance of being and having a good role model would be critical to my continued development. It raised the question: What's my reputation? If I *am* a role model, what messages am I sending to people? What am I known for?

My New Year's resolution that year was to better understand how I was perceived by others.

ACT 4: ROLE MODEL

Say and do what is right, and your reputation will soar.
People believe only the message of your behavior.

You might not realize your impact as a role model, but you can be sure that you're changing people's lives every day simply because you do the things you do. The result is your reputation. Tap your network to get diverse perspectives and listen closely to uncover the thing for which you are known. Consider your leadership potential and your character. How do you spend your time? Refer to *The 7 Acts of Leadership Workbook* to complete the reputation challenge, where you'll interview people from three aspects of your life: home, work, and community.

CHAPTER 7
PRACTICE, PRACTICE, PRACTICE

Meeta's words helped make me aware of my reputation. But how could I find out what other people thought of me? I soon chose some key individuals, guides, and courage coaches and asked them about my reputation. What was I known for? I asked for their suggestions for improvement, seeking to identify my areas of weakness. I asked them what they saw as my path and my potential.

Through face-to-face interviews with these people, I gathered information about my personal image, my expertise, my strengths. I discovered that I was known as an expert in project management. People came to me for advice on planning, organizing, team building, and conflict management.

It was reassuring hearing what they thought made me unique. When I asked what I could be doing if I wasn't in my current job, the answers ranged from park ranger to chief information officer. My leadership potential was high, but there were suggestions for improvement. These dear people made me aware of the unintended signals I was sending out without ever speaking.

No pain, no gain

Value comes from honest, meaningful dialogue, and this is where it got personal. My guides told me I was too quick to make a decision. That sometimes I came across as insincere, even patronizing. Ouch! I learned that leaders put people before the task. They admit when they're wrong and do something about it. It was time to say goodbye to "Callous Pallas."

I needed to focus my personal growth and development on having patience in decision-making and developing sincerity. I collected more information through more interviews, validating my understanding and clarifying viewpoints. I asked for examples and I got them.

I discovered my challenge to be a matter of authenticity. I needed a way to control my self-speak, the private conversation I have with myself in my head. I was only fooling myself when I would think, "I wish this conversation would end; it's a waste of my time," and behave as if I were engaged and interested. Faking that you're listening and faking that you care simply don't work. It's a source of miscommunication. Body language tells us what people are thinking. Even over the phone, transparency comes through in our tone.

Being the same inside my head as I appeared outwardly was the key to my authenticity. We can't demand trust from one another. We must develop it through authentic sharing. I added "authentic" to my character plan and began to treat my thoughts as real things. As for my quick decision-making, I decided to postpone addressing it until later. I needed to focus on one new behavior at a time, and it didn't take long for a challenge to present itself.

A glitch in the system

The conversation I was having in my head about Vince had nothing to do with authenticity. It was Thanksgiving Day, and I had a house full of family when he called. Vince was the programmer on-call for the holiday and the author of a mainframe COBOL program resulting in errors that were holding up shipments to 1,400 stores. We were hours away from the busiest shopping day of the year, and trucks were stuck on the docks at twelve distribution centers.

Vince was unable to decode the computer language and find the problem he'd created.

How had this happened without my knowing it? I thought every programmer on staff knew how to read a software program core dump. How did Vince become a senior programmer without this ability? Was he just trying to get out of doing the work because it was a holiday?

This incident arose before the days of remote access, and Vince was already at work. I was not controlling my inside or my outside voice. I genuinely wanted to poke his eyes out! I proceeded to express my thoughts at a volume exceeding the need for a telephone system. Overhearing the conversation was notice enough to my family that dinner was going to be delayed.

I turned the kitchen over to my husband and drove twenty minutes in to work, where I debugged the program code while Vince watched. I questioned why the test plan didn't catch the problem while he stared at me, paralyzed by fear. A few hours later, we sat in silence watching the program successfully execute in the production environment. I made calls up the corporate chain of command to report that the problem was corrected, knowing a full impact report would need to be filed the next day. I would be called to the proverbial carpet to explain, and I was dreading it.

After my family was gone, Rick and I washed the dishes and cleaned up the house. I reflected on my command and control style, my disregard for Vince's holiday sacrifices, and my uncaring approach. I recalled my commitment to caring about people, and I felt horrible about the way I behaved. I couldn't help but wonder how Vince felt.

"I wonder if Vince made it home in time for dinner," I said.

Rick was caught off guard. "You don't really care about that guy, do you?" he asked.

I paused before answering. My first instinct was to say no, but I was surprised by my answer. It was uncharacteristic of me.

"Yes," I said. "I think I *do* care about him."

I thought about what Virginia had told me about the key to her success and my promise to care. I was starting to understand what she meant. But on that day I failed horribly. Not only did I not care in my heart, I allowed my self-speak to control my behavior. I was thinking Vince was stupid, and it showed in the way I treated him. The reality was that Vince wasn't stupid; he was just afraid. He didn't want me or anyone to know he didn't have all the skills to do his job. This truly was a revelation for me.

The next morning, I set out to put my promise into practice. Ignoring the pile of emails and voice messages at my desk, I went straight to Vince's desk. I could see the fear in his eyes when he saw me coming. He braced himself for the worst.

So he was genuinely surprised when I thanked him for coming in to work on the holiday. I asked if he made it home in time to enjoy dinner with his family. I'm sure he thought I was on some medication. I apologized for my disrespectful behavior. Practicing everything I learned about difficult conversations, I kept the focus on me, being careful to avoid an accusatory tone.

I was honest about my expectation that he would know how to debug a "core dump." We both knew that, as a programmer, he needed to have this capability. I promised to teach him.

After my requisite song and dance to our corporate overlords, I returned to Vince's desk. Sitting side by side, we methodically analyzed the problem together. I not only took the time to teach Vince how to debug the application, but I set the tone for my expectations going forward. I wanted him to be successful in his career and be a contributing team member. I *did* care about him, but I was going to hold him accountable for producing quality work.

 Theory is good; practice is better

Climbing another rung on my career ladder, I was soon promoted to the job of system analyst. No longer managing people, my new job was to produce solutions, problem-solve, and work with my internal customers. I served buyers, inventory planners, store managers, and distribution center managers. I needed skills in analysis, problem-solving, collaboration, relationship-building, and conflict management. Navigating the politics of the organization became a necessary evil. I was learning the art of influencing because no one reported directly to me, but I still had to get things done. This is when I learned that organization charts are impressive in theory but façades in practice.

Eager to build my qualifications in business, I returned to school to pursue a master's degree in management. It would take two years of night school, but I was in no hurry. I was still learning as I prepared to be my own boss and run my own business. I could already see that navigating in a large corporation was suffocating my drive. I was a small change-agent in a large organization stifled by the status quo.

I also realized that the classroom is a valuable education in theory, but *practice* is the true teacher. The next two years were fun and eventful. As I picked up new ideas from the classroom, I immediately incorporated them at work. I experimented with strategic planning, various leadership styles, and change-management theories as if the workplace were my personal laboratory.

CHAPTER 8
COMMUNICATION IN THE DIGITAL AGE

One of my first homework assignments for my master's degree was to critique an external corporate communication. I figured it would probably be a boring quarterly earnings report. Instead, I learned a valuable lesson in how the digital revolution was changing communications inside — and outside — the workplace.

A brave new world

I woke up one morning to find a memo written by my boss's boss's boss, the company's Chief Information Officer, on the front page of the local business newspaper. The reporter described the memo as negative, autocratic, and harsh. I couldn't believe my eyes. I'm sure our CIO felt the same way. Still, I was thrilled to be delivered this A+ material on a silver platter, albeit at his expense.

Our CIO was getting resistance from his leadership team. After a frustrating meeting with his staff, he fired off an email to his staff, threatening them to get on board with a major company reorganization "or else." In the style of traditional leadership, he expected them to fall in line like good corporate soldiers.

I learned four things from our CIO's mistake:

1. Email is not the right medium for reprimands or inspirations. The risk of misunderstanding is far too great.
2. Never attempt to communicate during an emotionally charged moment. If it gets emotional, shut up.
3. It's always a good idea to offer a feedback loop so recipients have a way — other than going to the media — in which to reply.
4. Always communicate as if you're in public.

Later, I learned that the email was meant to be an inspirational gesture for some and a kick in the pants for others. I also found out that just because someone makes a communications gaffe doesn't mean he's a lifelong jerk. The person who shared the memo with the press was never identified, but rumors were rampant.

At the time, I was experimenting with my own leadership style, working on empathy and learning to better connect with people. I could relate to our CIO, and I actually felt bad for him. There are times when I can get frustrated, passionate, and loud. Sometimes even the best of us let our emotions get the best of us. Some of my emails have also been misunderstood. If I were higher up on the corporate ladder, it could've been *me* in the paper.

As a result of our email horror story, a corporate communications policy lockdown went into effect. Even our legal department got involved. Isolation became the flavor of the month. While executives issued restrictive new rules for using email, corporate soldiers ignored them.

The game had changed. There was a time when secrets could be kept in the boardroom. Key decisions used to be debated in hallways, and decisions merely confirmed for the record in meetings. Now, tactful messages about visions and goals replaced coercion as a communication best practice. Some of our company leaders began to use transparency as a weapon against political backroom deals and manipulation. It became harder for leaders who preferred to politick behind closed doors to use coercion, but the change was slow.

Always communicate as if you are being recorded

The implications of all this for me were that I needed to be deliberate and skillful in the use of any recordable communications. I employed transparency as my way of demonstrating authenticity. Imposing an email review checklist on myself helped me be more objective about how my message might be interpreted:

- Know the purpose and intended outcome of the message
- Be aware of when emotions are driving communications
- If emotionally driven, send the email to myself first
- Impose a "cooling off" period (sleep on it)
- Open the email the next day
- Read the email from the other person's perspective
- Consider the importance of the message and the risk of misunderstanding
- Listen to your gut
- Ask for coaching from guides
- Don't be tempted by the convenience of electronics

Writing down the purpose and intended outcome helps me predict people's reactions the same way that writing a goals statement helps me clarify my vision. The purpose of the exercise is to strip out the baggage and speak to the needs of my audience, not my ego. Email is best suited for fact-based information that needs to be pushed out to one or more people.

Email — and texting — is not an appropriate communication vehicle for any meaningful conversation.

When it came time to pick a subject for my graduate dissertation, I immediately gravitated toward my passion: strategic organizational change. I reached out to our CIO, Ron. Yes, the very author of that infamous email. I knew I was taking a chance when I went around my manager, her manager, and a director to get to this guy. I explained my school project to his administrative assistant, and she squeezed me into his schedule the following day.

My assignment required original research data. I asked Ron if I could collect organizational change-readiness data from his department of 1,200 people. He not only said yes, he signed up as my sponsor and invited me to his next staff meeting to explain my project.

Using our information-systems department as my research project was ideal. It had been several months since the email debacle, and Ron was still struggling to light a fire under his management team. He was open to new ideas, and I was full of 'em.

My findings and recommendations report described the current state of the workforce as resistant to change. People were set in their ways, not yet ready for a new way of operating. I offered options ranging from incremental steps to transformational strategies. Because of the risk of negatively affecting ongoing operations, I recommended waves of structural and systematic changes. To sidestep resistance and capture a quick win, I suggested isolating a self-directed dream team to test a small group concept focused on customer service. The joint business and technology team would operate outside traditional functional lines of authority.

Within weeks, I was promoted to a special assignment reporting directly to Ron. I took a chance, and it paid off. My new job was to work with an external consulting firm to spearhead these transformational department-wide changes. Suddenly I was living my dream!

🦉 Seek advice, listen, and reflect — but do what's right for you

All this time, I'd been on the lookout for a mentor, someone who could advise me on how to navigate the corporate system and share industry knowledge. Ron wasn't the female mentor I hoped to find, but he turned out to be much more of a coach than I ever expected.

For nearly six months, I met with Ron every Monday morning at seven. I came armed with a list of things to discuss, and he, of course, brought his list, too. I was surprised but delighted that we almost always covered my list first. He took his role of mentor and coach seriously. With both hands, he shoved me out of my comfort zone, and I soon found myself in front of hundreds of coworkers presenting our organizational change strategy. By including me in strategy meetings, Ron taught me how to collaborate with our vendors as partners. I attended executive-level meetings, where I saw how big corporate decisions were made.

Ron challenged me to expand my network to help build my reputation as an expert in my field. We had meaningful discussions about the differences between how men and women approach networking and the value of surrounding yourself with talent from inside the company and beyond. He taught me the importance of getting involved with professional associations so that I could mingle with experts in the field and get an industry-wide perspective.

I did not pick Ron as a courage coach, but he turned out to be just that. He was a mentor who freely shared his knowledge of the retail industry, and he encouraged me to think about my management style and leadership approach. I didn't always heed his advice, but I always respected it.

CHAPTER 9
ROCKY ROAD AHEAD

I was just gaining confidence in myself as a leader when my abilities were put to the test. Our change initiative at Kmart was cut short by a new one: downsizing. I was there to witness the first bloodletting during a Saturday morning budget meeting where Ron was terminated.

Suddenly, my courage coach was gone, replaced by Carolyn, a woman with a take-no-prisoners leadership style and a reputation as a "hatchet man." We were suddenly a team. Our mission was to cut costs, and that meant reducing headcount. She liked that I had eight years of experience working on various jobs throughout the department. I knew almost everyone, and she knew no one. My knowledge of our staff's capabilities provided Carolyn good insights as to who stayed and who would be let go. She was aggressively managing up and down the organization to get the cuts done as soon as possible, and I was her right-hand woman.

We were both experienced at managing pockets of resistance, and in just a few months we plowed through Kmart's internal politics. Twenty percent of our Information Systems staff was to be eliminated just months after Ron's departure.

On the Monday before Christmas 1994, I stood before forty managers crammed into a conference room designed to hold twenty. These were the same people I had worked with over the previous four months to collect years of staff performance ratings. We engaged in many late-night discussions about normalizing our employee-performance scores across departments. No one was surprised, but I could still see the fear in their eyes. They wondered if they were on the termination list or if maybe they'd been invited to the meeting because we expected them to do the dirty work of firing someone.

I wish I didn't care

It never occurred to me that I might struggle to address this group. I was confident our analysis was done fairly. Scheduling the layoffs just days before Christmas was outrageous, but that decision was out of my hands. I worked with a workforce transition and outplacement firm to ensure that terminated employees got the support they needed. Our surviving managers were paired with a consultant to help them carry out their orders.

On that morning, I was exhausted. I'd worked all weekend to make sure there were no mistakes. I checked the documents and made sure everyone had the information they needed to do the best job they could. I personally matched terminator to employee. Information Technology Security had the list to revoke system access, and Facilities Management was posted throughout the building to assist with staff exits and address any security issues.

I was ready for everything — everything, of course, except for my reaction. For months, I'd isolated myself from my network of friends to avoid spilling any secrets. My withdrawal prevented them from inadvertently picking up any clues from me about who was going to be fired. I couldn't afford any rumors. For years, they'd been my support system, the people I would go to when I had a bad day or when I needed to talk. I purposefully alienated them so I could get the task done. But the isolation took a toll on me.

I stood before this handpicked group, some of whom served as my guides. They were people I admired. Now they were looking to me for guidance. I had worked for and with all of them over the previous eight years. Together we shared long days and nights producing amazing results.

For a moment, I took comfort in reminiscing about a time in that same conference room when we were watching news about Hurricane Hugo traveling up the East Coast. As landfall predictions changed, we invented ways to override the transportation system so that truck drivers could get diapers and bottled water to the stores closest to storm victims as soon as it was safe. These people were part of my life, and I cared about them. I also cared about the people they would soon be letting go. This day would change all of our lives forever.

Standing before them, the reality of the situation suddenly hit me, and tears began to stream down my face. I didn't have a tissue, and nobody offered me one. The room was silent, the tension suffocating. Not a word was spoken. They stared back at this person who'd started her career as "Callous Pallas" now struggling to gain her composure.

Finally, I managed to break the silence. "I asked you here this morning," I said, "because you've been selected to execute one or more terminations today." I saw relief on some faces and anger on others. A couple of managers refused and left the room. This left me to coordinate reassignments. I found it interesting that they refused; it never occurred to me that refusal was an option. But I had little time to contemplate their points of view.

By two o'clock in the afternoon, the terminations were over. I rounded up my things and headed back to my office thinking about the managers who refused to execute the firings. Carolyn would not be happy. Deserters would most likely be axed, as well. Now that my task was complete, I thought that I, too, might get the ax. I wondered if my walking papers were waiting for me at my desk.

The halls of the building felt eerily silent, as if everyone had gone home. It was a long, lonesome walk through wing after wing of Kmart's world headquarters. I wandered past cubicle farm after cubicle farm and trudged downstairs to my office in a remote corner of the campus. Jacqueline was waiting for me outside my office door. It was nearly nine years since we'd started our careers together on the same day — our first "real" jobs. She even helped talk me into accepting the position as special projects assistant to the CIO.

"It'll be fun!" she said. "You'll get to hang out with executives. It'll be good for your career."

Jackie was my peer and my only confidant throughout the ordeal. She came to help me at five o'clock Friday night when I got the order to carry out the firings. We worked together all weekend making sure there were no mistakes in the paperwork and rehearsing the execution plan. She helped me reserve meeting rooms and draft communications. Together we met with Kmart's security team to manage the facility and technology risks. The logistics plans seemed limitless.

We could see the regret and the relief in each other's eyes as I unlocked my office door.

"Sorry about losing it this morning," I said. "It all just hit me at once."

"It was good," she said. "It showed you're human and everyone needed to see that. What else is there to do?"

There were voice mails, emails, and notes everywhere, but I just didn't have the strength to face them. We were exhausted. I was disgusted with the way things played out and rued the day I took the job. So this was price of leadership?

I locked the office door, and we went home.

Returning to work the next day with a heavy heart, I realized that things would never be the same again. I could never return to the way things were. My relationships with my colleagues had been irreparably damaged.

Coping with a new corporate culture

During the previous few months, I'd been privy to Kmart's corporate decision-making process at the executive level. Prior to my special assignment, when Ron was still in charge, our top brass would weigh the pros and cons of an issue and conduct a level-headed debate, followed by meaningful dialogue and a consensus vote.

Without Ron, Kmart's new culture was more like a cruel competition of empire-builders, egomaniacs who cared more about golden parachutes than about the golden rule.

My dissertation on organizational change was now just a memory. My recommendation included leadership strategies to develop a culture of accountability and customer responsiveness. That vision was lost. Instead, I'd just participated in the destruction of a workplace civilization, and now it was time to rebuild based on a new set of rules for navigating the political landscape.

After being trapped in secrecy behind closed doors for months, I returned to a department of peers who were going through the change process I'd imposed upon them. I was going through it myself. The terminations left the department with fewer people to do the same amount of work. There was no denying it.

Carolyn and I never talked about changing the way we did the work. We only talked about eliminating staff — a lesson I took forward as I planned future change projects.

Some people were frustrated and angry, some were in the bargaining stage. Others were hopelessly struggling with a new reality. Very few had reached the acceptance stage. Our organization was unstable, and people were still trying to grasp their new roles. Most of my colleagues saw me as a traitor, and the trust I'd worked so hard to build could no longer be taken for granted.

Carolyn proudly rewarded me with a double promotion. I would manage Inventory Management Systems, the heart of the supply chain. A few months later, I was moved to Store Systems and then to Human Resources. There didn't seem to be a fit for me in the new corporate culture.

Rebuilding the organization seemed like a daunting task, especially since I'd lost faith in our leadership team. I felt a cavernous pit in my stomach. Where do I fit into this company, I wondered. What are my goals now? Can I keep working here and stay true to my character plan? I was lost, once again seeking a vision. I needed time to reflect, time to find a new path.

Spend your time on the things that matter

I was emotionally exhausted by the pressures at work, as well as the pressures at home. After a lifetime of smoking, Ma was now suffering from emphysema. We realized she was also suffering from dementia when her apartment manager called one day to let us know things weren't quite right. Ma had called maintenance about a problem with her stove. When the manager arrived, all the cooktop burners were set to "high" and Ma didn't know how to turn them off. He felt she was a fire risk. He was right.

We immediately moved Ma to live with my sister Mary, who became her primary caregiver. Ma was struggling with Alzheimer's and no longer recognized her own children. As her health deteriorated, so did Mary's ability to cope. Watching our mother die was a heartrending and overwhelming process.

Meanwhile, it was once again time for a divorce — this time from Kmart. It had been nearly ten years since the company had given me my first "real job" as a COBOL programmer. My identity was tied to my job, and my coworkers were a big part of my life. Leaving them would be hard, and I didn't want to get escorted out of the building, like I knew I would be once I gave my notice. Keeping in touch with people wasn't easy back then, and it was important to keep your Rolodex up to date.

I decided to quit on my terms, and once again I prepared an exit strategy. I made a list of twenty-eight people I wanted to say goodbye to and plotted out where they sat in the complex. A team of trustworthy coworkers served as my lookouts in case my boss or security came looking for me.

I packed my things on a Thursday night, and early Friday morning, I left my resignation sealed in an envelope on my boss's desk. I then began visiting the people on my list, saying my goodbyes and quickly moving on to the next person. By 10 a.m., my boss was on the hunt for me, but my team skillfully navigated me around Kmart's maze of cubicle farms. By 11, the word was out and the people on my list were waiting for me to arrive. No one had turned me in. At noon, I strolled into the HR director's office and asked for my exit interview. She smiled and offered me a seat.

"You know everyone in the building's looking for you, don't you?"

I knew.

Nancy and I chatted for about an hour. We'd worked together on Kmart's controversial downsizing project, and we had our memories. She thanked me for stopping to see her and finally walked me to the door. We hugged goodbye, and I was on my way. It was time to focus on my family.

While I helped Mary cope with Ma's illness, I started to ponder my next career move. My dream of having my own consulting business was visible on the horizon, but not yet within reach. For one thing, I lacked consulting experience.

I worked on my résumé while sitting with Ma, who now no longer recognized me. We barely spoke a word because there simply wasn't anything to talk about. It wasn't long before we moved Ma to a nursing home. The person I knew as my mother was long gone from the body of this frail woman tethered to an oxygen tank. She had a distant look in her eyes — a blank stare, and I wondered if she was frightened or happy to soon be meeting up with Pa.

Ma died on December 1, 1995, the day after my thirty-eighth birthday.

Later that month, I started a new job as project manager with the Big Six consulting firm of Coopers & Lybrand.

With both of my parents gone, I was now officially an orphan. My siblings and I had just become the generation of elders; our time was running out. I couldn't help but reflect on my legacy, and I asked myself again and again, "What do I want to be known for?"

CHAPTER 10
PAYING YOUR DUES

Being a consultant can complicate things at work. Instead of having one boss, you have two: the client organization and the professional-services firm. When I joined the Big Six, I was immediately assigned to a financial-services client managing a computer-system–development project.

My first day at the firm was spent at the local office. I picked up my firm-issued laptop and downloaded documents from the local area network. I installed the firm's proprietary project methodology software. My boss, George, gave me a brief overview of the project and introduced me to some of my team members. I would be assigned a mentor to help get me acclimated to my new role.

 Serve the customer first

I spent the rest of the day with Ryan, the sales guy. Ryan had been my staffing supplier at Kmart, and it was because of him that we were working together again. He took the time to explain how the project was sold, the original proposal, and resulting contract.

My job was to execute according to the contract. The objective was to get the customized system built using client business resources, my firm's client-server resources, and a team of mainframe programmers from a competing staffing company.

My client was Matt. He was my single point of contact for a project originally scheduled to last ten months. My first day at the firm was my last full day at the office. For the next five years, I spent my days traveling from one client to another, leaving home every Monday morning and returning every Friday night. Suddenly I was a road warrior.

It didn't take long for me to wonder where my loyalties aligned. Was I supposed to serve the best interests of my client — or my firm? My client was understaffed, and I could see that Matt wouldn't be ready to accept support of the new system by the proposed launch date. If I waited to raise the issue until closer to launch, Matt would have little choice other than to extend the contract. This would result in additional revenues for my firm. But if I raised the issue early, my client would have choices and could take action to move internal resources around. However, this would mean a lost opportunity for the firm. I didn't know what to do.

I posed the question to Ryan, although I knew he wasn't objective. His sales commission would be affected by how I handled the situation. "If you do what's right for the client," he said, "it'll be the right thing for the firm."

Ryan felt that honest and transparent communication leads to a long-term relationship and ultimately continued revenue. I liked his philosophy. From then on, I was able to make the right choices, even when no one was looking. The approach aligned with my values.

It was because of Ryan's mentoring that I discovered the concept of *servant leadership*. The term, coined by Robert Greenleaf, describes a leadership style in which a leader serves first and leads second. I found the philosophy helpful in allowing myself to let go of being the decision maker. I came from an organization that expected managers to make decisions and direct workers. Now my job was to provide options and guide my customer in making good decisions. My mantra became "I advise, you decide."

I was now in the service industry; decision making was no longer mine. My job was to be the best I could be at bringing together the assets of the firm, information, and human talent to serve the needs of our clients.

I was lucky to have Ryan in my network, and wished I had more people like him. The professional-services firm was vastly different from the corporate culture at Kmart. At the firm, there was a sense of urgency about delivering value. Everyone tracked their time so that customers could be invoiced. If you weren't "billable," you'd better have a good story about how you spent your time.

I went from a social organization that invited everyone to meetings to a firm where attendees had to be justified. Clients couldn't be expected to pay for a consultant sitting idle at a meeting. Results were king, and I was in the right place, moving closer to my entrepreneurial goal. This was my laboratory for entrepreneurial learning.

After several weeks at the client site, I returned to the office to meet my mentor, the only woman on the Detroit management team. Little did I know Gina would someday become my business partner.

Each consultant was required to attend forty hours of training a year. The organization's commitment to learning was one of the main reasons I took the job. Gina listened to my goals of being the best project manager I could be, of learning the business of consulting, and of building a reputation for delivering quality results.

She suggested I take classes in project management, facilitation, and the firm's system development methodology. We even plotted out a two-year development plan. Through Gina's network, I now had access to some amazing talent, and I needed to leverage it. At long last, I had found another courage coach.

Deliberately building your reputation

I knew that promoting my credentials was part of being an effective consultant. It was something I needed to get used to if I was going to go out on my own someday. During my brief time between jobs, I took a pulse on my reputation by conducting a few informal interviews. What was I known for, and what was my potential? Where should I focus my learning development?

I learned that people who knew me found me to be trustworthy, approachable, confident, and results-driven. These characteristics aligned with my character plan, but I also needed to be known as an expert in my field. I needed credentials beyond my education, credentials that differentiated me in the workplace.

At the time, certificates in project management were rare, yet well respected. I began studying for the 700-question Project Management Professional exam, and I submitted my application to the Project Management Institute. Some of my coworkers were interested in getting their certification and, before long, I was facilitating an informal study group with consultants from across the firm. My circle of influence had gone from local to national.

Leading that internal study group accomplished three things:

- Established me as an expert in project management within the firm
- Expanded my network of guides
- Helped me become certified as a project management professional

All these benefits came into play later when I started my own consulting business. To sustain my reputation as an expert in project management, I also contributed to the project-management community through volunteer teaching and speaking engagements.

It wasn't long before Gina was promoted as the only woman at the firm's Center of Excellence, blazing yet another trail. Her promotion left the local office in need of a female engagement manager. Following the path Gina made for me, I stepped into the role and began managing multiple project teams across several clients. Mentoring was part of my job, and I was assigned a handful of consultants. I was also expected to be 80 percent billable. That meant 32 hours a week had to be billed to a client, any client.

It was just me and seven men on the leadership team. Back then, technology consulting was in its heyday. The year 2000 was fast approaching, and the hype about computer system crashes fueled our business. My project-management credentials came in handy. Project management was being recognized as a critical factor in the quest to save the world from billions of lines of computer code that couldn't process a two-digit year of '00.

I was one of those COBOL programmers in the 1980s who coded two-digit date calculations into my programs. I understood all too well the risks. Back then it was expensive to store data and, as a result, we only captured and stored the last two digits of the year. We calculated ship dates, arrival dates, and number of days outstanding based on simple math. We never anticipated handling a negative date. The year 00 minus the year 98? Error! The result would be an abnormal end, or as we called it, an *abend*. Fear rocked the information-technology industry, and professional-services firms raked in the money.

My days at Coopers & Lybrand were action-packed. I drove from client to client, checking in on project teams and facilitating meetings. New hire interviews were conducted on Fridays, after the weekly managers meeting. Breakfast and dinner were spent meeting with mentees. Lunch was a granola bar in the car. In the evenings, I answered emails and worked on client proposals.

The job market was hopping, and newly hired consultants were jumping ship to chase bigger and better offers. I was confident in my ability to coach project managers in planning and delivery execution, but I was having trouble connecting with new hire mentees.

My mentees were a new breed of workers. These young professionals understood the need to add value to the client during agreed-upon hours, but they wanted balance in their lives. The line between work and home life had blurred. Remote access put the workplace in the hands of the worker, and we could work from anywhere. The Digital Age had arrived. As long as the work was getting done, my mentees didn't see the value in showing their faces at the client site every day. They wanted to be judged on results; their loyalty wasn't to the firm, but to their own future.

And who could blame them? Our firm was in the midst of a merger with Price Waterhouse, and the uncertainty left my appeals for loyalty empty. How could I persuade the next generation of consultants to stay on board, at least through the end of the engagement? Why was I struggling to connect with them?

Lessons across generations

I had successfully influenced the lives of my nieces and nephews, who now ranged in age from 11 to 28. I'd established guiding principles of lecturing for myself, and they were push-pinned onto my corkboard above my phone in my home office:

- Spend as much time as possible listening
- Get right to the point without being judgmental
- Hold the conversation in confidence
- If it gets emotional, shut up

I pondered my work challenge and reflected on my personal coaching successes. The thought occurred to me that one of my family members could very well be working with me or for me someday.

Some of my nieces and nephews were already in the workforce as young professionals, and they faced many of the same challenges as my work mentees. I'd learned so much from listening to my family that I was certain I could apply it to my work situation.

How would I mentor and coach my nieces and nephews if they were colleagues at my workplace? It was an interesting question that caused me to consider a new perspective. I took out a clean sheet of paper and wrote down the following:

- Let them know that I care about their success beyond their job at the firm
- Find every opportunity to match them with opportunities that align with their ambitions
- Set expectations that sometimes you need to "pay your dues" to get experience that's foundational to preparing for the next opportunity
- Introduce them to people so they can expand their networks
- Join their networks
- Inquire about their goals (personal, work, and community)
- Push them to try new things
- Generate opportunities for them to market themselves
- Invite them to meetings so they can model appropriate leadership behaviors

Up until this point, I had failed to mention any of this to my mentees. I was focused on how to submit time sheets, expense policy guidelines, and client issues. In the all-consuming job of engagement manager, I'd forgotten my own lessons of leadership.

It took time, energy, and focus to be a coach, as well as a mentor. But the effort paid off in the short term, as well as the long term. Today I have lasting relationships with some very talented and capable people, and my network is rich in capability.

At the intersection of my work mentor role and my role as an aunt, I found life solutions that enabled me to be the best coach I could be. Through reverse mentoring, my nieces and nephews helped me to understand younger points of view.

By now, my life was filled with coaching and mentoring family and colleagues, who called at almost any time of day or night. It was Sunday afternoon when Jackie called.

At the time, we were information technology consultants on the road, traveling to client sites every week. We were road warriors. We went our separate ways in the 1990s, taking project-management jobs at rival consulting firms, but we often tapped each other for network resources and problem-solving ideas. When discussing the intricacies of inventory management, distribution centers, and store systems, we had our own tribal language — a language filled with acronyms and code words for everything.

Over the years, I'd gotten a reputation for being a project-management geek and Jackie for solving complex process problems. We were both very good at bridging the gap between business user-speak and technical geek-speak. It wasn't long before Jackie had earned her stripes and was getting airlifted into troubled client sites to repair runaway projects. This was one of those times.

"Jim's sending me out to the West Coast in the morning," she said. "I need ideas on how to save this client relationship. The president of the company tossed our project manager out of the warehouse on Friday. The receiving system isn't working, and trucks are backed up outside the shipping docks."

I needed the other side of the story. "What's your project manager's story?" I asked.

Jackie explained that the guy had quit and that he wasn't returning calls.

"Did Jim tell the client to expect you?" I asked. "What are you going to do if they won't let you on-site?"

Jackie was frustrated. She was tired of cleaning up after her stupid colleagues who were probably making more money. She had more airline rewards than she could use in a lifetime. If she took a vacation, she took it at home.

"Jim will call there in the morning," she said, "but I'll already be in the air. Apparently, the client is threatening litigation, and Jim needs legal to be on the call. This is the first phase of a multimillion dollar engagement. I'm supposed to save this phase and convince this guy to keep us on for the next phase. If they don't let me in the building, I'll come home and start working on my résumé!"

While Jackie was telling me her story, I searched my folder of canned lectures and coaching notes. I was sure I'd written some profound statement that would magically transform her defeatist attitude into unbridled enthusiasm. Although the notes had mostly been collected during sessions with my nieces and nephews, they were coming in handy for work situations, as well.

I read to myself:

 Manage to the best case, plan for the worst case. (Too late for that.)

 The door to change opens from within. (I doubted the client or Jackie wanted to hear that.)

 Be a friend, listen, then shut up. (This was pretty good, but not good enough for the situation.)

Code word: PxPUP

I had nothing, but I still felt compelled to help. Jackie had always been there for me, even during the dark days of mass terminations at Kmart. I needed to be there for her. We sat in silence for a few moments. I was thinking about what my mother-in-law had told me years before — Virginia's secret.

It was worth a shot.

"OK, wait," I said. "Forget about the project for a minute. Just forget about it. Tomorrow you're gonna sit down one-on-one with the client and just listen to his story. Really listen to him. Get to know his fears. Don't defend your company or make excuses for your project manager; just listen. You have to really care about him as a person first; the rest will take care of itself."

It was so compelling, I even believed it myself.

There was no doubt that Jackie needed courage to pull this off. On one hand, it could end up being a career-limiting move, followed by months of testimony in court. On the other, it could result in a recovered engagement and possibly lifelong relationships, maybe even a promotion. It was a risky approach, but it was the only advice I had to offer.

Before I hung up, I said, "You better pack an extra pair of underpants because if this guy doesn't throw you out, you'll be spending more nights than you planned."

From that moment on, "pack an extra pair of underpants" ("PxPUP" for short) became our secret code for "show you care."

ACT 5: CARE

Share this emotion if you dare.
It costs nothing if you truly care.

Caring is the most powerful of *The 7 Acts of Leadership*. It requires being authentic, using time wisely, taking a coaching approach and setting boundaries. You can't fake it. Being true to your character shows through to your followers. Leaders express concern by taking the time to genuinely connect with people. They honor them by actively listening. Just because you care doesn't mean you should give away authority or compromise your values. It took me a long time to figure this one out. I really didn't care about anyone else through my seeker years and into my pathfinder years. It wasn't until I changed my thinking about caring that I truly became a leader. *The 7 Acts of Leadership Workbook* offers an assessment measuring the degree to which you demonstrate caring behavior.

JOURNEY OF A TRAILBLAZER

CHAPTER 11
COMING HOME

While Jackie's newfound success showed she really cared about her customers, things were rapidly changing with my job. The merger of two multinational consulting firms resulted in PricewaterhouseCoopers, the largest professional services firm in the world. Internally, we were faced with a new organizational structure, realignment of the workforce, and stricter conditions of employment. I'd been managing organizational change for our clients, but I hadn't experienced it myself since I'd fired nearly 200 people from Kmart six years earlier. I knew there had to be some value in living through this major transformation at PwC. Experiencing organizational change from the inside would be a good experience for me, and I planned to stick around to seek out learning opportunities.

Survival at the firm meant embracing change, so I fell in line with my colleagues, learning a new customer-relationship management system, realigning my teams to match up with a new human-resources model, and taking any training I could get approved. I tried to avoid office politics by focusing on client service and my ability to be billable — or as we called it, *billability*.

While the firm's partners were busy fighting over who was in charge, I was protecting my reputation and contemplating my next move. I was trying to find my role in a completely new organizational structure. It was like betting on the horses. Who was going to win? There were rumors that our technology line of business would be absorbed by management consulting. That didn't bode well for my direct leadership, as their high-tech knowledge base might not be valued in the new organization. The only certainty was uncertainty, and I was feeling the daily pain in conversations with my mentees and clients who wanted continuity.

My new "mentor" was a woman partner from Texas who flew to Detroit to meet with me and fifteen other high-potential women at the firm. Donna's mission was clear. She encouraged us to stay through the transition and commit to getting on the partner track. The firm had what they called "inclusion expectations," and, as women, we could help her meet a quota. But Donna didn't even pretend to care about us. During a two-hour breakfast meeting, she intended to identify partner candidates and weed out dissenters. It was the first time I'd met anyone at the table, and I was pretty sure it would be my last.

There was a moment when I considered the partner track, but breaking through the glass ceiling was no longer important to me. My experiences as a woman on the local management team were valuable, but my priorities had changed. I was watching my home life slip away, and I wanted more control over how I spent my time. Thanks to my new "mentor," I realized I was no longer learning. It was either be a partner or step aside and make way for someone else.

I filed my incorporation papers and waited.

🦉 You're the boss of yourself

I didn't want to believe what I just heard. "Your ethics are getting in the way of us making money." Was George serious? I waited for the expression on his face to melt into a smile. He was obviously frustrated with me. It was September and our office needed to meet a sales goal by the end of the year.

I had just wrapped up a multimillion-dollar software implementation engagement at a client where I spent two years managing a consumer goods distributor through a transformational process involving strategic visioning, software package selection and implementation. There would be additional opportunity to sell services next year. It was time for the organization to absorb changes brought on by the new technology. The client's focus had to be about surviving retail busy season, period.

My job as an engagement manager was to manage client relationships and oversee projects. I was expected to uncover follow-on business opportunities. When I started with the firm four years earlier, the values were different. Selling services was about discovering a match between the client need and the services we offered. We were in the business of making a profit, but we were also adding value to our customers.

The next engagement would require the attention and time of the client's management team. Putting a team at the client site before the end of the year would be of no benefit to the client. After a few months of paying the bill, the CEO would be angry about paying high-priced consultants to sit around. Kevin would be angry with me, not the firm. My experience taught me that clients align with people, not companies. It was my reputation and, yes, these were my ethics.

"If you pushed, do you think you can convince Kevin to buy now?"

Kevin was the CEO of a fast growing company and we joked that we had a love-hate relationship. Every month he hated to pay the bill, but he loved the work we did. I challenged him to be a leader of change, and he challenged me to invent ways to ready each and every one of his staff for the new system. "There will be no casualties; these are the people who got us here. Find a way for them to survive the journey."

I considered my boss's challenge. Could I convince the client to buy consulting services that would add no value to him but satisfy the firm's revenue goal? It might have been my ego or my competitive nature, but I got excited at the thought of the win.

I told George yes. I could sell it.

I watched George slide into his chair behind his desk, his shoulders relaxing and his attention turning to his next task. His body language was dismissive. He was done with me.

I sat studying him as he wrote in his planner. He was oblivious to the impact my decision would have on my reputation. He didn't care.

But *I* did. I could not be true to myself and take advantage of my client for the benefit of George, or the firm.

"Yes, George," I said. "I could sell it...but I won't."

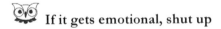 **If it gets emotional, shut up**

George shot up from his chair and hollered down the hall as I walked away. "What exactly is your relationship with Kevin anyway?" he said. "I thought there was something going on between you two."

That was the last straw.

I was pissed, embarrassed by his insinuating my relationship with Kevin was less than professional. Anger welled up inside me; I wanted to fight. But I kept on walking, letting George's question hang unanswered in the air. Still, I couldn't help but wonder what my colleagues thought as I stormed past their offices.

Breathe, I told myself. I recalled my brother's advice about how men make sense out of their worlds.

My brother John explained "sex-thinking" to me on Day Two of my first menstrual period. John and I sat on the battleship gray paint-chipping back porch steps of our childhood home. "You need to understand how guys think," he said. "Every moment of every day is spent thinking about sex. Unless we are actually having sex, we are scheming to have sex. We make sense out of the world from a sex perspective." At age sixteen, John was an authority on sex.

Sex-thinking was my rationale for how George reached his conclusion that my refusal to sell the client a project doomed for failure must have something to do with me being a woman.

I was beginning to see why buyers were suspicious of consultants. Potential customers treated me with suspicion and my time at the firm gave me insight into why. *Don't worry about if they really need the service; just sell it so we can make our sales numbers.* It was easy to see the connection between a professional services firm's thirst for greed and the demise of American institutions whose leaders followed the advice of their trusted advisers and sank millions of dollars into technology projects that brought operations to their knees. The firm had a blacklist of customers we were told not to reference in sales proposals because project failures resulted in litigation.

I was confident my decision was the best for the client, for the firm, and for me. Had my values changed? Or had the firm's culture changed as a result of its recent merger? I didn't know. It was time for me to test my leadership potential and become my own boss.

It was time for me to blaze my own trail.

I proved I could be successful as a consultant working for the largest professional-services firm in the world. I was confident in my ability to manage and lead myself and others. It was time to make it on my own. I just needed to know what "make it" meant to me.

I started my career renewal with a review of my vision, goals, network, and reputation. My primary goal was to get off the road and uncover work in my local community. Detroit has a rich manufacturing history, and for the past two years I'd been assigned to financial-services clients. I needed an entry into manufacturing.

My knowledge of packaged software along with my retail and distribution experience had me well-positioned for supply-chain consulting work. I understood distribution, warehousing, order processing, and inventory management, but what I didn't have was practical experience with manufacturing systems. In the Motor City, this was a real credentials gap.

Working at the Big Six consulting firm taught me that letters after your name open doors. A certification in supply-chain management from the American Production and Inventory Control Society would get me a credential. Membership in APICS would expand my network. It meant passing five separate exams, and I immediately went to work studying.

I was completely in charge of my schedule. I could've sat around the house and watched TV, but I filled my time with personal development and start-up activities. I read *How to Succeed As an Independent Consultant* and drafted a business plan modeled after a project I did in grad school.

To maintain my reputation as an expert in project management, I volunteered to develop training for the local chapter of the Project Management Institute. Ironically, PMI had just added *professional responsibility* as a new element to its standards guide. The results of a global study determined that successful project manager competencies included professional responsibility behavior, a topic that had previously been ignored. With that in mind, I designed and delivered training on the topic.

There were emotional highs and lows. I felt liberated by my decision to leave the firm but fearful of failure. However, my carefully crafted goals helped keep me focused on my success. "Believe in yourself," I told myself every day. "People will believe in you if you believe in yourself."

A few months after I left PricewaterhouseCoopers, a former colleague and mentee invited me to help him establish a project-management office at Volkswagen. My independent consulting career was underway.

The Lighthouse at the end of the tunnel

Within the year, Gina quit the firm and we met to explore a partnership. We'd been colleagues for five years, and our ethical standards and philosophies aligned.

We started developing product ideas on a clean sheet of paper. We were "eating our own dog food," using the same consulting approach with ourselves that we'd used on our clients. It was hard work. We considered our strengths and weaknesses, examined opportunities and threats, conducted market research, and created value propositions. It was a creative process that could not be held to a timeline.

By the time I got my certification in supply-chain management, we had a business plan, a marketing strategy, and an operating agreement. We would offer consulting skills training and coaching services. Our plan was to capture a niche in the market, targeting the industry we'd just come from. After all, consulting skills were our strength. We knew it was true because former colleagues were calling us for coaching advice.

Gina and I named our company Lighthouse Consulting Partners — *where consultants go for guidance*. Our lighthouse logo reflected our new company's goals. We wanted to be known as a Michigan-based company, and the image of a lighthouse was appropriate for a state surrounded by water. Our goal was to *teach* clients, not *tell* them. When we walk away, we said, we wanted our clients' employees smarter and their businesses stronger.

Gina and I went into business to make a difference, to strengthen our community, and to do what's right. We joked that having ethics would be our competitive advantage — but behind our laughs were scars. We really meant it.

We designed a logo, printed some brochures, and started tapping our network. We gave away pens, notepads, and pencil bags to get the word out: We're open for business. Our enthusiasm was infectious, and our story was compelling. Who better to teach service providers how to be consultants than two former PricewaterhouseCoopers consultants? We incorporated our coaching method into the consultant's community model, and our first course was born.

Critical to the success of our unique business model was our freedom to pursue independent and partnered opportunities. We needed to trust each other's intentions — as well as our ability to deliver — in order for it to work. This arrangement required courage to take risks and to hold each other accountable. It was critical not only to believe in ourselves but to believe in each other. This we did. And as partners, we invariably became each other's courage coach.

ACT 6: HAVE COURAGE

Face your fears and take the lead,
With good judgment you will succeed.

Courage isn't just taking that first step; it's making things work. It's about having the hard conversation that's easy to avoid. Courage is about looking in the mirror and recognizing, accepting, and doing something about your fears. It's the "fire in the belly" that drives you to change and to lead change. Sharing your fears with a courage coach demonstrates your maturity in leadership. This activity is not an assessment of your current state, but a plan of action. *The 7 Acts of Leadership Workbook* offers an action plan checklist.

CHAPTER 12
LEAVING A LEGACY

Working from our homes, Gina and I were able to start our business with a minimal investment for business cards, marketing brochures, and a website. Evaluating my network, I was satisfied with the guides I'd found in my professional-services experience. But now it was time to look to the community for sales opportunities, as well as entrepreneurial mentorship.

At first, it wasn't about giving back to the community; it was self-serving. When I worked for PricewaterhouseCoopers, I had access to our Centers of Excellence, research teams, and subject matter experts. If my computer broke down, it was immediately repaired by a highly skilled college intern who grew up in the Digital Age. If I wanted to think through an idea, I could enlist any one of my colleagues. I was spoiled by the talent that surrounded me on a day-to-day basis, and now it was gone.

The isolation of entrepreneurship can be comforting to an introvert, but it's unsettling to an extrovert like me. Our success depended on me learning to fix my own computer and expanding my network. I set out to uncover the capabilities of the untapped members of my network and to meet new guides — people from whom I could learn business ownership and share sales leads.

Searching for guides at the Project Management Institute, American Society of Training and Development, American Production and Inventory Control Society, Toastmasters, and the Institute of Management Consultants resulted in only a few deliberate invitations to my network. These organizations offered industry-best practices, but I couldn't make a connection with the quality of leaders I needed.

In search of...

I was gaining an appreciation for how hard it is, in the absence of leadership, to create that mysterious "connection" with people. I bounced from one group to the next, listening to presentations, eating rubber chicken, and waiting for inspiration.

Then I discovered the Michigan Council of Women in Technology. This was a group of women seeking mentors for other women. Sandy, the founder and president of MCWT, explained their mission and the background of her leadership team. She was a retired entrepreneur, and we talked for over an hour as she recalled the isolation she felt as a woman in a predominantly male field.

The "connection" was made. Although I was inspired by Sandy, my connection was with her vision to promote opportunity for girls and women in a male-dominated industry. Finding myself energized, I pondered what was missing from the other organizations.

All of the associations could offer me an avenue for networking, sales leads, and industry-best practices. But they didn't have a vision for change. Their purpose was to transfer knowledge, be the keepers of best practices, but I was seeking to be a part of a cause, something that was bigger than me.

My reward for my volunteer time with MCWT was the gift of influence on my community. It was an honor to be part of such a worthy cause, one that brings opportunity to girls and women pursuing careers in technology. The resulting relationships have been priceless, and the experience was my greatest lesson in leadership.

I was serving on the mentoring and event-planning committees when everything suddenly screeched to a halt.

Diagnosis: Cancer

The pressure in my abdomen was unusually uncomfortable. I wondered if something was wrong or if I hadn't scooted far enough down the exam table. My family doctor is a witty woman with a dry sense of humor. We usually traded lighthearted jokes, but this time something was different. As she finished my pelvic exam and I slung my butt back onto the center of the table, I could tell something was wrong.

"I don't like what I'm feeling," she said. "I want to send you for tests."

We both knew that I had fibroid tumors on my uterus. I had regular ultrasounds for years, and there had never been an issue. But this time was different. I scheduled tests for the following week and went home and started educating myself. I no longer had to go to the library to do my research. Everything I needed was on the World Wide Web: fibroid tumors, ovarian cancer, false positives.

As each test result came in, my symptoms pointed more and more toward ovarian cancer. If it was true, the prognosis would be bleak. Weeks went by, but it seemed like forever. I wanted to work, but I felt paralyzed. My logical brain was trying hard to get on with life. I tried meditating to recapture my positive attitude. But it was all for naught.

I tried my best to think positive thoughts, but that couldn't stop the tears from streaming down my face. Why was I crying? What was I afraid of? Dying? Suffering? My failure to leave a positive imprint on the world?

Then I asked myself, "What are the chances it'll be cancer anyway?"

Thoughts, as I often say, are *things*…I tried to convince myself that there was hope. My mother's sister died of breast cancer, but that was different. There was no history of ovarian cancer — or was there? I rummaged through the family genealogy documents. Mary and I had meticulously documented every finding. My mother's grandmother, Anna Haas, died on November 3, 1913. Cause of death: uterine cancer.

After weeks of blood tests, ultrasounds, and CT scans, I met with a board-certified surgeon at the Karmanos Cancer Institute in Detroit. This was the third doctor I'd seen in eight weeks. This was the guy my second doctor said he would send his wife to if she were ill. In spite of all the test results, I was still hopeful — or maybe I was in denial.

Dr. Moore's physical exam was much more thorough than the previous two. The silence in the room was heavy and palpable. Rick sat by my side, and I was grateful he was there to help me listen to what the doctor said. I felt violated and very sore as I struggled to sit upright after the exam.

"Your cancer," said Dr. Moore, "is *blah blah blah blah blah*…"

My head was reeling. My *what?!* How could he use that word?! How does he know it's cancer? It could be a fibroid cyst gone wild. "Tell me again," I said. "Why you think the mass is a threat to me?"

The doctor explained that my CA-125 blood test came back extremely elevated above the normal range. But he assured me that the blood test alone was not a predictor of cancer. False positives were high, especially in stage one cancer. He was really pissing me off. "Why is he jumping to conclusions?" I asked myself.

But I remained outwardly silent, trying hard to listen.

I knew that the CA-125 blood test was unreliable, but it was the only thing the medical community had to diagnose ovarian cancer without surgery. I was high risk, and I had all the symptoms. But I wanted to know my options. Was this something I could treat with medication or a change in lifestyle?

"How large is the mass?" I asked.

Dr. Moore stood before me with his fists clenched side by side to demonstrate the size of my tumor.

"It's partially blocking your colon."

He said I had no other options and recommended surgery as soon as possible. My last doctor had talked about using a surgical scope to minimize the invasive nature of surgery, and I wanted to understand what Dr. Moore meant by "surgery." An incision, he said, was the only way to go. That way he could examine all my organs and properly assess my condition. In other words, he wanted to know what stage my cancer was at and what other organs it affected.

My nephew Johnny and his fiancée, Jenny, had just graduated from med school. They were due to be married in a few weeks, and I was *not* going to miss the wedding. It would be the happiest day of their lives, and I didn't want it tainted by cancer. I postponed the surgery until after the wedding.

I kept my diagnosis a secret and enjoyed their celebration as if it would be my last. Once the newlyweds headed off to their honeymoon, I broke the news to my siblings.

In the days leading up to the surgery, I was consumed with making sure I'd reached my life goals. I had a sense of urgency about everything around me, yet I was paralyzed to act. I became reflective as I considered my life's accomplishments. Had I been the role model I'd hoped to be? Did I make a difference in people's lives? Could people depend on me? Was I trustworthy? Did I face my fears? Did I learn from my childhood mistakes? Was I a good wife? What would my family say about me when I'm gone? What was I known for?

I wondered if the kids would reminisce about eating MRE (meals ready to eat) out of a bag on Manitou Island, calling out mountain lupine flowers on hikes, watching the sunrise in the fog at Montauk Point, shopping for shoes, or calling me for a quick lecture. I wouldn't want them to forget about all those profound short statements that I saved for them over the years.

"Leave the kids my pearls of wisdom in a book," I wrote in my planner. I didn't know how much time I'd have. I'd know more after the surgery.

Post-Op

To this day, I don't understand how I could've been blessed with such a positive outcome. Five days after a complete hysterectomy, I left the hospital with the good news I was cancer-free. After a week of recovery at home, we returned to the surgeon's office for a checkup.

While we waited for Dr. Moore, the nurse practitioner explained what happened. "The surgeon made an incision from your pelvis to your navel."

I sat and listened in silence. "Really?" I thought to myself. "Tell me something I don't know."

"Then he proceeded to remove your intestines and abdominal cavity organs and place them on your stomach and chest."

That was an image I'd rather forget.

"That's how he examines the organs searching for signs of cancer."

She continued to explain that I had a benign tumor the size of two fists and the rest of my insides were cancer-free. The doctor removed the tumor, my uterus, and ovaries and replaced my intestines and organs.

"How does everything get back in the right place?" I asked. The nurse practitioner told me not to worry and assured me that it all finds its way back to its proper place. Dr. Moore came in the room, conducted my pelvic exam, and wished me a good life, leaving me in the very capable hands of his nurse practitioner.

Throughout my six weeks of rest and recovery, I became anemic. My red-blood-cell count was low, and my energy levels even lower. Dr. Moore considered a blood transfusion, but he wanted to see if I could recover on my own. About all I could do initially was answer emails and thank people for their flowers and gifts.

It took almost six months, but eventually I got my groove back and my energy returned. All along, I cherished my good fortune and reflected on how my cancer scare had changed me forever.

Our little business was doing pretty well. We established our partnership in 2000 and soon found ourselves adjusting to customers reeling from the emotional and economic impact of 9/11. The strength of our relationships sustained us through the hard times, and our ability to work well with customers enabled our continued success.

Our catalog expanded to over twenty courses in project management, business analysis, and soft skills. We found our niche by providing custom solutions to organizations struggling to deliver technical solutions with global teams. Our secret has always been to care about our customers and to help them achieve their goals.

Gina and I brought on two additional partners to help support our West Coast operations. We expanded our market reach through partnerships with larger training organizations. We tapped our network to help satisfy the demand for experienced trainers and consultants. Sharing our success with the team enabled us to grow the business while still maintaining a healthy work/life balance.

While I recovered from surgery, I slowly pieced together an outline for my book, which soon began to consume my thoughts. But before I knew it, business as usual filled my days, and the book project began collecting dust. A couple of years went by, and I landed a project-management coaching gig in Kalispell, Montana.

At the end of the workweek, I took my book outline and my folder of lectures and drove up to Glacier National Park. By the time I got there, the visitors center was closed, so I took a walk down to the water. There, I found a group of painters on the beach with their canvases and their oil paints, fast at work capturing the setting sun over the mountains. I stood on the beach and took in the scene. The water was so calm and so clear, I could see the orange, tan, and brown stones at the bottom. I felt right at home.

I remembered my trip to Yosemite and the Grand Canyon years before with my sister Mary, where I'd found the courage to reinvent myself.

This was my first trip to a national park by myself, and it was the perfect writing retreat. A few years earlier, Rick and I had been to East Glacier, but we never made the trek to the western side of the park. Although I wished he'd been there to share in the scenery, I was grateful for the time alone to dedicate to my book. As the sun began to set in the west, I got back in my car and drove along the lake to historic Lake McDonald Lodge.

👀 Time is the only commodity you own; use it wisely

Long ago, I had set a goal for myself to write a book, and for years I let business as usual get in the way of my dream. It wasn't until I *made* time that the journey of finally writing this book began in earnest. In that magical place along the crystal-clear waters of Lake McDonald, far away from the crazy day-to-day demands of the rat race, with no cell phone and no email access, I began to leave my legacy.

The idea of writing this book was born out of my affection for my nieces and nephews, the same ones I had taken to the Grand Canyon, had hiked with to the top of Mount Washington, had taken surfing in San Diego. I cared deeply about them all, and I desperately wanted to leave them a legacy. Not a trinket or money or a trust fund. But a way of living, a way of leading. That night, in the mountains of Montana, this journey began.

I reflected on the choices I had made, both good and bad. I considered the point in time when I stopped living day-to-day and began to truly envision a future for myself. Studying the other visitors as they sat by the massive fireplace in their comfortable chairs, I wondered if my story would inspire them. Were they here taking time to dream, visualize, and set goals for themselves? Maybe they are in that place I've been in many times before: looking for courage to take the road less traveled.

My gift to these travelers, strangers from around the world and my friends and family will be my life lessons, a guide to being the best you can be.

Inspired and emboldened by my surroundings, I picked up my bags and climbed the stairs to my room. There was much work to do.

And I was glad I'd packed an extra pair of underpants.

ACT 7: LIVE RIGHT

Leaders are driven by a belief about what is right.
Never letting values out of their sight.

Consider the impact of your leadership style on the people in your life. Are you the same at work as you are at home? Do you take responsibility for yourself and set expectations for acceptable behaviors? Do you have the same expectations for yourself as you do for others? Living a leadership lifestyle doesn't take any special skill or knowledge. It only takes desire. How will you take your learning forward to inspire the people in your life to join you on your life's journey? *The 7 Acts of Leadership Workbook* provides you with a lifestyle self-assessment.

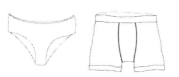

LEADERSHIP IN THE DIGITAL AGE

The need for trailblazing leadership has never been stronger. Worldwide changes in global economic, political, social, and cultural systems are redefining value. The 21st century is so different from the era of mass production that it requires a new mindset. We are blazing a digital age trail. The world needs leaders to invent new ways of creating value and new ways of working.

There's no road map for today's leader. There are no role models. Communication vehicles are immediate and transparent. Coworkers, support teams, and suppliers are thousands of miles away and right next door. Rules about right and wrong were written for the Industrial Age, when patents could be protected and national boundaries could be defended. Now determining the right thing to do is a personal choice, not a cultural norm.

We are the role models of the future. We're blazing a new trail, a narrow path for future generations to make worn. Our footsteps will lay the groundwork for future superhighways. Footpaths will take followers to places of interest; the main track and the spur trail are both part of the leader's journey.

It's up to us to help ourselves and others through the transformation from an industrial age to a digital age. Our leadership will help coworkers, family, and friends find a way forward.

Leadership begins with knowing where we're going while helping others articulate their dreams. Finding the connection comes when the desired state turns into a believable story that has meaning to people. Having the courage and endurance to manage resistance will make the difference between immediate progress, slow incremental change, or failure.

What will your role be in redefining leadership in the digital age? Are you a seeker of change, a pathfinder, or trailblazer?

THE 7 ACTS GUIDE

The 7 leadership behaviors listed here are a guide to living a leadership lifestyle. The associated workbook activities can be found in *The 7 Acts of Leadership Workbook*.

Act 1: Know where you're going
Visioning and goal-setting enables realization of dreams
Activities: Vision Statement and Goal-Setting

Act 2: Broker Capability
Designing a network of talent requires knowledge of people
Activities: Character Plan, Network Map and Network Capability

Act 3: Connect
Making connections depends on a clear vision and a believable story
Activity: Communication Assessment

Act 4: Role Model
Deliberately selecting and being a role model defines character
Activity: Reputation Challenge

Act 5: Care
The key to leadership
Activity: Show You Care

Act 6: Have Courage
Bravely taking action after thoughtful consideration
Activity: Courage Plan

Act 7: Live Right
Choices made when no one is looking
Activity: Lifestyle Assessment

LASER LECTURES

The owl — a symbol of wisdom

1. Learn to say "That's unacceptable"
2. If it's important, leave nothing to chance
3. You cannot be, until you see
4. Surround yourself with people you admire
5. Never take your network for granted
6. We teach people how to treat us
7. Stereotyping is never the right thing to do
8. You'll never have time unless you make time
9. You don't win trust, you earn trust
10. The only thing you can change is you
11. Care enough to take the time to know people
12. People are listening
13. Theory is good; practice is better
14. Always communicate as if you're being recorded
15. Seek advice, listen, and reflect — but do what's right for you
16. If it gets emotional, shut up
17. Manage to the best case, plan for the worst
18. The door to change opens from within
19. Be a friend, listen, then shut up
20. Hold conversations in confidence
21. Deliberately build your reputation
22. You're the boss of yourself
23. Time is the only commodity you own; use it wisely
24. Pack an extra pair of underpants

More Laser Lectures at www.MichellePallas.com

ABOUT THE AUTHOR

Michelle Pallas has served the information technology industry for over 30 years. Prior to joining Coopers & Lybrand in 1994, she held various positions at Kmart corporation and became an entrepreneur in 2000 when she started her own consulting and training business. Today she is President of Michelle Pallas, Inc. and Managing Partner of Lighthouse Consulting Partners.

Pallas holds a bachelor of science in computer-based information systems and a master's degree in management from Walsh College of Accountancy and Business Administration in Troy, Michigan. She became certified as a Project Management Professional in 1998 and achieved a Certificate in Integrated Resource Management from the Association for Operations Management in 2000. Pallas completed the American Society for Training and Development Train-the-Trainer program in 2003. She achieved her Competent Communicator award from Toastmasters International in 2013.

She takes her role as coach seriously and has influenced the lives of many colleagues, clients, community members, and family. Pallas lives with her husband in metro Detroit, where she supports the development of community leaders through her work with nonprofit associations. She is a founding member of We Build Character, where she established community-based mentoring programs for young professionals and high-potential leader candidates. As past Vice President of Strategy, Pallas was instrumental in expanding the reach of the Michigan Council of Women in Technology in their mission to promote opportunity for women and inspire girls to pursue careers in technology.

Contact Michelle at Michelle@MichellePallas.com